"Scripture makes it abundant [...] very center of God's heart, and reaching out to [...] of His kingdom is as profoundly Christian as it gets. Every child is designed to be nestled within a family, and it is unacceptable for any child to live as an orphan on this planet. Reaching out to orphans in their affliction (James 1:27) is a mandate for all of us. While not everyone may be in a position to adopt, we should honor those who can and rally around them to lift the burden, financially and emotionally, in support of this kind and loving act."

—DR. WESS STAFFORD, president emeritus,
Compassion International and
author of *Too Small to Ignore* and *Just a Minute*

"To engage the world at its most hurting is a venture of great complexity and cost. Doing so wisely and well demands thoughtfulness, continued refining of approach, and a compassion rooted deep in the love of God. *KnowOrphans* offers all of these with frankness, insight, and humility."

—JEDD MEDEFIND, president, Christian Alliance for Orphans and
author of *Becoming Home*

"I first learned of Rick Morton through reading his previous book *Orphanology*, which he coauthored with Tony Merida. From then until now, I have considered Rick to be one of the leading thinkers, advocates, and activists in the evangelical orphan-care movement. His latest book, *KnowOrphans*, is true to form. Evangelicals are frequently criticized as believing adoption is the primary solution to solving the global orphan crisis. In *KnowOrphans*, Rick not only methodically and winsomely demonstrates that this is indeed not the case, but also with careful and biblical wisdom demonstrates that the Bible actually provides holistic answers to those complex solutions. If you want to learn how you, your family, your church, and your organization can better address the global orphan crisis, get yourself a copy of Rick's *KnowOrphans*. You'll most definitely be better prepared to address the needs of orphans everywhere."

—DAN CRUVER, president, Together for Adoption; coauthor of *Reclaiming Adoption: Missional Living Through the Rediscovery of Abba Father*

"Rick Morton is tackling the tough issues of orphan care and adoption in a straightforward and biblical manner. This much-needed book will help individuals and churches better *KnowOrphans,* their plight, and how we can better address the issues they face on a daily basis. *KnowOrphans* will be a much-used resource for churches and any Christian that cares about orphans and how we best minister to them in their distress."

—JOHNNY CARR, vice president, strategic partnerships, Help One Now; author of *Orphan Justice: How to Care for Orphans Beyond Adopting*

"Rick Morton lives out a gospel-centered passion for orphans and families. This book delivers that passion with practical steps for you and your church to minister to the little brothers and sisters of our Lord Jesus, orphans in your neighborhood and around the world. Read this book and give a copy to someone who needs to see the blessing of following Christ in ministering to children in distress."

—RUSSELL D. MOORE, president, Ethics & Religious Liberty Commission, Southern Baptist Convention

"Two words stood out as I read through *KnowOrphans: informative* and *inspiring*. This is a book that addresses with beauty and balance the world of adoption. It is biblical and practical. It also is an honest book that addresses both the ups and downs of this important issue. Prepare to be blessed! Prepare to be challenged!"

—DANIEL L. AKIN, president, Southeastern
Baptist Theological Seminary

Rick Morton is one of the most credible, knowledgeable, passionate voices for orphans and vulnerable children in the world today. This book is compelling! With every page, I felt the need to give more, do more, and pray more. Read this! Then, as God leads you, jump into the journey with all your heart."

—TERRY MEEUWSEN, founder, Orphan's Promise,
cohost, *The 700 Club*

"*KnowOrphans* is a practical, how-to guide for believers ready to engage orphans worldwide. The simple fabric of the book cannot be missed—ultimately the hope of orphans is not our engagement, but in the gospel of Christ. Rick engages the reader with honesty, humor, and humility. Although the evangelical orphan-care movement is currently being attacked, Rick gives a constructive critique that encourages us to realize the urgency of the orphan crisis, while not compromising on integrity. It is Christ exalting to wrestle with this content and be motivated not by the need but by the gospel."

—HERBIE NEWELL, president/executive director,
Lifeline Children's Services, inc.

Other New Hope books
by this author

Orphanology:
Awakening to Gospel-Centered Adoption
and Orphan Care

coauthor, Tony Merida

Know Orphans

Mobilizing the Church for Global Orphanology

Rick Morton

NEW HOPE
PUBLISHERS
Gospel-Centered. Missions-Driven.

BIRMINGHAM, ALABAMA

New Hope® Publishers
PO Box 12065
Birmingham, AL 35202-2065
NewHopeDigital.com
New Hope Publishers is a division of WMU®.

Library of Congress Control Number: 2013955336

Interior designer: Glynese Northam

ISBN-10: 1-59669-399-1
ISBN-13: 978-1-59669-399-9

N144108 • 0314 • 3M1

Dedication

To Denise

I get to write and speak, but you are the real hero of this

family's story. I still can't believe you said yes, but I am

thankful every day that God has given me the

gift of sharing life and love with you!

Contents

Acknowledgments

No project like this comes about out of the work of one person. So many have helped, encouraged, and contributed along the way, and I would like to thank them personally.

The greatest thank-you is reserved for my wife, Denise. You are a strong, beautiful gift from God. A visionary with a heart for Jesus and the fatherless that inspires and challenges me. Thank you for loving me and teaching me.

I must thank my kids for their unwavering love and support. Nastia, Nicholas, and Erick, I am so proud of who each of you is and who each of you is becoming. I am so thankful God gave us the gift of each one of you. We are so blessed to have incredible stories of how God brought each one of you into this family, and I can't wait to see how God continues to write those stories into the future!

I am forever indebted to the people of Faith Baptist Church and Temple Baptist Church, who have given me the opportunity to serve you as a pastor and to lead you to care for the fatherless in new and greater ways. Much of what this book shares with others comes from ministry alongside you. Thank you for being the people of God who care for the "least of these" to the "praise of His glorious grace" (Matthew 25:45; Ephesians 1:6).

The Christian orphan-care community is such a special group of people, who give freely to help each other care for orphans without regard for personal accolade. I have been so blessed to get to know so many godly, gifted people who have shaped my heart and mind through countless hours of conversation as well as collaborative work. While I cannot begin to thank you all individually, I am thankful for each of you.

I would be remiss without expressing my deep gratitude to the team at New Hope Publishers. You all have become family to me! Andrea Mullins, thank you for believing in this project enough to champion it. Joyce Dinkins, you are the *best* managing editor on the planet. Thank you for praying me through and believing I could get this on paper even when I was not sure. To Melissa, Maegan, Tina, Kathy, and everyone else on the team, I say thank you for everything. Your passion for the gospel permeates your work.

Finally, thank You, Jesus. Without Your adopting grace, this book really has no meaning. This is written because You are a Father to the fatherless and a defender of the defenseless.

Foreword

A FEW YEARS AGO, WE EXTENDED OUR FAMILY. MY WIFE, KIMBERLY, and I adopted four kids from Ukraine, and then a year later, we added a little boy from Ethiopia. We went from zero kids to five! When people ask us why, I typically respond by saying, "We were motivated by theology, not biology." Our understanding of what God's Word says about adoption and the fatherless caused us to repent of our indifference and inactivity, and to reorient our lives. In the middle of this new journey, we experienced the blessing of having close friends walk with us and remind us of these truths, and one of them happens to be the author of the book you hold in your hand. Rick has taught me much about the theology of adoption and orphan care, and was one of the first adoptive parents that I knew and watched.

A few weeks ago we extended our driveway. I'm a pastor of a church plant, and much of our ministry takes place in homes. And one of the homes is ours. When our concrete man was finishing, he asked our kids if they wanted to put their hands in the wet cement and write their names there. Of course they took him up on this offer!

Each morning when I walk out to the car, I see the imprint of these five pairs of little hands. They make me think of so many things.

The most pressing thought is that we have a short time with our children. They are like wet cement. They should come with a sticker, "Yours for a limited time only," because they are with us for short time. It's like you go for coffee, come back, and discover they've grown three inches. When I see these little hands, it makes me think of my need to parent them well in our short time together. Then I think about how challenging parenting is, and I try to change the channel in my mind!

These little hands make me think of other hands too. I think of millions of orphans who live in some of the most unimaginable conditions. Abuse, neglect, disorders, abandonment, fear, doubts, grief, despair, illness, hopelessness, and emptiness are just a few common experiences of the world's orphans. I think about little Russian girls; each may never have a dad hold her hand as he takes her out for dinner and a movie, or later give her hand in marriage. I think about little Ugandan boys; each one may never have a dad teach him how to drive, shoot a basketball, or hold a door for a lady. I can't think about these little hands very long either. I want to change the channel.

But we can't change the channel. This is the fallen world in which we live. We have an orphan crisis. And while we can't change the channel, we can change the picture.

You see, our lives are like wet cement also. Our brother James tells us not only to care for orphans in their affliction (James 1:27), but he also tells us that life is short (James 4:14). What will we do with our short lives?

Let James 4:14 and James 1:27 talk to each other, and listen to the conversation. What do you hear? You hear something like, *Don't waste your life. Make it count. One way to make it count is by loving orphans.* There are a whole lot of ways to waste your time, money, and energy, but one thing is clear: caring for orphans isn't one of them.

God is called "Father of the fatherless" (Psalm 68:5). That is astonishing. One way you could introduce the God of the Bible to the world is with this title. And God calls His people to imitate Him.

Orphan care is warfare; but it's a war worth engaging. It's one sure way to not waste your short life.

The question is, How should we care for orphans? Obviously, you can pursue adoption. But while more families should be considering local and international adoption than currently are considering it, adoption is only one of many ways to *do* James 1:27. Not everyone is called to adopt. Not every child is available for adoption. But every believer is called to do something.

So I'm glad Rick has written *KnowOrphans*. We need to know how we might live out this biblical vision of orphan care in our short lives. You have in your hands a book from a guy who can teach the Scriptures faithfully, who is an adoptive parent, and who knows many of the key orphan-care leaders nationally and internationally. He has seen firsthand what can happen in churches and countries when people practice wise and compassionate orphan care. And he has some important and hope-filled counsel about what could happen in the future.

Those hands on the concrete also make me think of something else. They make me think of the day when there are no more orphans. When the King returns, peace and righteousness will dwell. God will dwell with His people forever in a land apart from orphans, human trafficking, poverty, and AIDS. Until we bow down before Jesus, and reach out hands in praise and honor of Him, who didn't leave us as orphans, let us bring a glimpse of the future into the present—by doing what we can to see a world with no more orphans.

Tony Merida

So Here We Go . . . Again

THANKS FOR PICKING UP THIS BOOK. THE ODYSSEY between the writing of *KnowOrphans* and *Orphanology* has been quite a thrilling ride. When we left off our story in Orphanology, we were a family of four expecting soon to become a family of six. Well, a funny thing happened along the way. One of the girls said no, and as an almost adult, that was her legal right. The other said yes and, just shy of her 15th birthday, came home and joined our family. We have made a move to another ministry context and have seen God do some pretty great things in both our ministry and our family. Life hasn't always been easy or even fun, but Jesus never promised us it would be. What we have learned is that He is enough.

It has been an amazing gift to have a front-row seat to see what God is doing in and through His church in the global orphan-care and adoption movement. I feel like I have grown and learned so much since coauthoring *Orphanology*. Yet, in a much greater way I feel like we are all just getting started in seeing what God is up to through the global orphan-care and adoption movement. Things have changed and evolved rapidly. It has been a really crazy ride. I am continually glad that God is in control!

I sense the worldwide church is on the verge of an awakening. When God begins to move and wake up His church, it is something special. The Book of Acts is filled with stories of movements of

God. Church history is too. I think we are living on the edge of something amazing, and God's heart for the fatherless is at the center of it. It's been amazing to hear from leaders all over the globe confirming that the signs of this awakening are everywhere in the global church. Indifference is giving way to gospel-centered action, and God is getting much glory.

A lot of this book is about knowing orphans, not because they are *unknowable* but because they are *unknown*. They are voiceless. They are out of sight and out of mind. At worst, orphans are treated as a social blight or, at best, they are ignored by the mainstream of society. Yet God says He is their defender, and He is awakening His church to join Him in that work. In caring for orphans, He is teaching us something about Himself as a redeemer, His gospel as restoring grace, and His Son as the coming and re-creating King.

The best part is that this revival of concern isn't confined to one part of the globe. God is moving in a noticeable way all over the world on behalf of the fatherless. In John 14:18, Jesus said to us, "I will not leave you as orphans; I will come to you." Because He didn't leave us, we can't leave them. To not leave them, we have to know *who* they are, *where* they are, and *how* to help them. What if getting to know them and how to help them could help us form a God-sized vision of how to end the orphan crisis? Impossible? Remember what Gabriel told Mary, "For nothing will be impossible with God" (Luke 1:37).

I have spent most of my ministry studying adolescents, including many hours analyzing their development. I think the life cycle of a developing human being can be a useful metaphor to help us understand how movements tend to develop. As with any maturing person, in movements there are also predictable stages and issues at each phase of maturation. I have come to think that the global orphan-care movement has reached *its* adolescence. We are not in our infancy, nor are we just beginning to explore the world as preschoolers. We understand a little about the world we live in and are confident in the basics. We are still a little unsure of who we are and don't really know everything that we need to know to function well for the rest of our lives, but we are gaining on this.

Like teenagers, we are learning more about ourselves, and we are learning more about God. We are discovering places where we are missing the mark, errors in our perceptions of the world and ourselves. We are facing criticisms that cause us to review our convictions and actions. We are mature enough to be self-reflective and to respond to criticism with introspection and adjustment if needed. Whatever happens, dealing with the criticism—though it may be uncomfortable—isn't unproductive. It is part of growing up.

The change and growth that comes during adolescence is fascinating as well. While this growth is certain, it is anything but steady and comfortable. Laws, terms, and even practices change in orphan care and adoption, and those changes, too, can be uncomfortable and even unpredictable. What we can be certain of is the love and unchanging nature of God, and we can be thankful that He is a defender of the defenseless and a Father to the fatherless. He guides us on our path.

So, I hope you are ready to go along for the ride during this adolescent phase (awkward growth spurts and all), as we dive into understanding a little more about ourselves in the global orphan-care and adoption movement and how we can grow into the future.

Over the years I have loved ministering to adolescents, being part of shaping their promise for the future and the unbridled opportunity that takes place in those years. The teen years are a magical season of life to walk through with a child. It is a time of defining identity and watching potential begin to change into capacity. Increasingly, the global orphan-care and adoption movement is defining its identity and identifying its best practices.

The journey has not been easy, and the rest of the way promises to be no less challenging. But by God's grace, we can care for the world's orphans for His name's sake. I am excited to explore how that can happen throughout the pages of this book, and I am grateful to take this journey with you!

Chapter 1

This Wasn't Always My Heart

A DECADE AGO, OUR INTRODUCTION TO THE WORLD of global adoption and orphan care was much like that of many families. After years of struggling with infertility, my wife, Denise, and I began to sense God drawing us toward adoption. Well, not exactly. Denise began to sense God drawing us toward adoption. I, on the other hand, was completely disengaged from the idea. I mean, sure, I wanted to be a dad, but *adoption? Really?* It hadn't even occurred to me that our journey to parenthood wouldn't be like everyone else's, and when it did, I freaked out.

I had a million questions. I had heard tons of stories about failed adoptions and crazy legal situations involving adoptive parents and birth parents. It was hard enough dealing with infertility. Could we deal with the twists and turns of adoption? I questioned everything. I fretted over the cost and the complexity of adoption. I wondered how I would feel about an adopted child. Today these questions, quite frankly, seem silly to me, but at that moment they were as huge as any questions I had ever faced.

Still, Denise was insistent. She was operating out of a deep conviction that God had given her about our need to pursue adoption. She and God were patient with me. I'm not sure why I didn't share her passion. Maybe it was a male thing. I guess I had just never thought much about it. So, for a while, I was quiet and worried. Then, I worried out loud. Worrying aloud was not very helpful to anyone (and I imagine more than a little annoying to people around me). But I had to do something. So I was driven to look for answers in the most reliable place I know, the Scriptures. As a pastor and professor, I had counseled others to look to Scripture for wisdom for years, and I had embraced it for myself. Why should this matter be any different? I was tardy, but I got there. It seems obvious now, but at the time I was confused. I needed clarity. I needed God's voice.

I tried to take a systematic approach as I began to look at what the Bible has to say about the subjects of orphan care and adoption. This is probably not the course that everyone would take, but it made sense to me. I am not sure what I expected to find. I mean, I knew of some seemingly disjointed fragments from the Bible about orphans and adoption, but I had never studied either topic with any depth. In all the years of Sunday School, sermons, and even seminary, I had never heard anyone teach what the entirety of God's Word says about these things, let alone undertaken a systematic study myself.

What I found rocked my world! I hadn't noticed that there was much more of a point to God's plan for caring for the fatherless than showing His benevolence. To that point, I certainly hadn't seen anything eternally significant in His call to care for orphans, much less understood that it unfolded in a way that pointed both to His character as Redeemer and to His plan of redemption in the gospel. But it was there, and suddenly it was exploding off the pages of the Bible right before me.

On top of that, I had never appreciated all that Paul said about adoption in the New Testament. Perhaps I had been blinded by my own practical view of adoption. Previously I hadn't thought much about it. But now that I was, I was thinking differently about the questions that flooded my mind such as, *Can I love an adopted child with all of myself? Can we afford to adopt? What if our adoption leads to heartache or disappointment? What if*

Experts who have studied transnational evangelism have helped us to understand the complexity of crossing cultural barriers to share the good news of redemption in Christ.

our child suffered from some brokenness that we could not fix? What I saw as I studied Paul's writings on adoption was that God is an adoptive Father. He is *my* adoptive Father. He is the adoptive Father of all who have repented and followed Jesus. In Christ, I am the adopted heir of the Most High God. And I found myself grateful that He had shown none of the hesitation in adopting me that I was showing about adopting a child!

Wow! My doubts began to melt.

I don't want to oversell my understanding or my confidence at that point. It's not like God just flipped a switch for me, and I stepped from the shadows into complete understanding. The truth took a little time to form roots, but the conviction that adoption and orphan care came straight from the heart of God was rather immediate.

While that initial time in the Word didn't answer all my questions, God gave me enough confidence to take the next step. Time, reflection, and experience have worked together through God's Spirit to develop a much deeper sense of these truths now, but even in the beginning of this journey, the Lord gave me a glimpse of Himself that both humbled and motivated me. Denise and I were going to adopt, and what a ride it has turned out to be!

IGNORANCE ON FIRE

As I have talked to many people involved in Christian orphan care and adoption, I have found so many unique and special stories. For us, the journey to understanding and responding to God's heart for orphans began with adoption, but it has become so much more.

When it came to adoption, we were "ignorance on fire." We knew that God had put this in our hearts, but we had no idea where to start. In a previous state where we lived, I had some interaction with the Baptist Homes for Children, so we called up the Kentucky Baptist Homes for Children to begin the adoption process. We knew we were called to adopt, but we had no idea what sort of adoption to pursue: domestic or international, open or closed, foster-to-adopt or private adoption. To us, it really did not matter. All we knew was that we were open and ready. So, rather than waiting until all our questions were settled, we started walking through the process and trusting God to work out the details. Looking back, I can see the providential hand of God all over each step we took.

He led us to a social worker named Barbara. I cannot possibly tell you how blessed we were by her or how much God used her in our lives and our journey. Don't let me make it sound too romantic or simple. Barbara put us through the ringer. In addition to our home study, she had us go through the full state-mandated training to become foster parents. She had us attend workshop sessions on everything from medical issues in international adoption to fostering attachment with an adopted toddler. She gave us a bibliography of books on adoption that was as extensive as some of those I faced in my PhD program (and she gave pop quizzes!). I must confess that at the time I thought she was a bit of a taskmaster, but in the years since, I have been so grateful for her guidance and preparation.

One of the convictions that our experience with Barbara taught me is the need for education and preparation for transnational orphan care and adoption. Experts who have studied transnational evangelism have helped us to understand the complexity of crossing cultural barriers to share the good news of redemption in Christ. Like the process of sharing Jesus in other cultures, we must acknowledge that adopting and other forms of orphan care in nations that are not our own cause us to cross cultural barriers. To be effective, we must prepare by acknowledging, respecting, and accommodating these differences. Barbara had us read extensively to begin to understand our child's culture of origin and to prepare us for bridging the gap in and through the adoption process.

BUMPER BOWLING — OR, HOW GOD GUIDES

One thing we learned (and it has been reinforced to us in countless ways) is that God's heart is for the fatherless, and He will guide those who truly seek Him through the often confusing and difficult task of caring for orphans in the global context. Ten books couldn't contain all the things we have experienced over the past years in adopting and caring for orphans. God is so good and, as my dear friend Herbie Newell, executive director of Lifeline Children's

Services, often says, "If we think we love these precious children, we have to remember that our love pales in comparison to God's love for them and for us."

When I think about how much God loves the orphans of the world, I am literally moved to tears. Denise and I have been privileged to see and experience the providential hand of God as He seeks to protect vulnerable children all over the globe for His name's sake through His church. What we have witnessed has strengthened our faith and increased our resolve to be part of God's agenda to care for the fatherless across the entire world. It blows my mind that He uses ordinary people to do extraordinary things. He is using my family, and He can use you. Let me give you a couple of examples from our story of how God works.

God knew the heart of the social worker He gave us and, looking back, we can see how it was all part of His plan. Barbara and her husband had served for many years as international missionaries. Her dedicated heart for the gospel and for the nations resonated with us. God had placed her and her passion for the nations in our lives at just the right time. We began to sense that transnational adoption was the path that was best for our family.

Early on, one of the flyers we received from the Kentucky Baptist Homes for Children featured an announcement about their adoption program in Ukraine. We had no connection to Ukraine. In fact, I'm not sure that I could have found it on a map. Still, something about that flyer drew both of us. God began to consume our attention with Ukraine over the next few months. It seemed like everywhere we turned, that little part of the former Soviet Union or someone from it was waiting for us. God is great about working this way—gently nudging those who are seeking Him. He was ordering our steps even when we could not see it in the moment.

At the same time we began the adoption process, God opened an opportunity for me to begin a significant parachurch ministry with several guys with whom I had been close friends for years. Not so coincidentally, one of them had just adopted two daughters from—ready? *Ukraine*. God placed me back into a consistent relationship with this dear friend with whom I had lost regular contact. At a key time, God used my friend and his family to encourage, inform, and even steer us through many steps in the Ukrainian adoption process.

I tell you this story not because I am trying to influence you to adopt. In fact, I am quite confident that there are many people who will read this book who cannot or should not adopt. My motivation is simply to say that I am confident that if God is moving you toward adoption or any other form of orphan care, He will order your steps. I have often compared our experience to bowling in a bowling alley that is set up for children. It was like having those little bumper rails put up to prevent you from throwing a gutter ball. That's how so much of both the adoption and the orphan-care experience felt to us. No matter how often we began to drift toward the gutters of doubt or confusion, God just kept nudging us back into the alley of His plan for us.

If God is calling you to adopt, He will accomplish it. If God is leading you to care for the fatherless across the globe in some way other than adoption, He will accomplish it. We look at the task and often see it as too big or too complex. Those are the very circumstances in which God shows up and shows off for His glory and His namesake.

Another story comes to mind as an illustration of how God shows up and shows off. After we came to sense that God was leading us to adopt from Ukraine, we jumped in headlong and started taking steps to do it. Would it surprise you to learn that not everything was easy?

When I contacted the Christian adoption agency our social worker recommended we use to begin applying for their Ukraine adoption program, I was shocked at their response. The lady I spoke with at the agency spent most of our hour-long conversation trying to *talk me out of* adopting from Ukraine and into going elsewhere. No matter how I protested, she persisted in talking to me about going somewhere "easier." The conversation really confused me. Were we hearing God correctly or was our conviction about Ukraine just something we had imagined? We prayed for clarity, but we felt jolted.

Days later, I attended a conference and represented the seminary where I taught. Denise traveled with me as a sort of minivacation. Our school had a booth in the exhibit hall to connect with prospective students, and I spent most of my time in between conference sessions visiting with prospective students. One day, Denise came by to join me for lunch. I was engaged in a conversation, so she just waited in the booth. A young man came by the booth to inquire about the seminary, and they struck up a conversation. She noticed his name tag: *Slavik.* She asked where he was from. "Ukraine," he answered.

Denise told him that we were considering adopting from Ukraine. When he heard that, he leaned in and gave her an incredibly intense look. He said, "Before I came to America, I used to help families adopt in Ukraine. It can be difficult. I will pray for you, and if I can ever help you, please call me." With that, he gave her his business card and walked off.

Crazy! I remember her telling me about it over lunch and thinking, *Hmmm, Ukraine again. It seems like it is around every corner.* The fact is, we hadn't seen anything yet.

Just a few days later, we found ourselves halfway across the country in a meeting set up by my new business partner to consult with the people from the agency that facilitated the adoption of his children. They were meeting because his family and the agency were working together to begin an orphan-hosting program. God didn't waste our eavesdropping in that meeting either. We were crashing the meeting because my partner wanted us to meet someone who could give us a different view of the Ukrainian adoption process, but God had a larger purpose. After we spent some time learning about Ukrainian adoption, their attention turned to discussing their orphan-hosting plans. Denise and I just listened as they went over what seemed like dozens of details. At one point, the agency director brought up the need for translators. She said, "I think I have everyone lined up that I need to translate for us except one. There is this guy that used to work for us, but I have lost touch with him and can't find his contact information. I think God wants him here. His name is Slavik."

Denise and I gasped! *Seriously?* Denise pulled out the business card and gave it to them. Yes! It was the same person! Coincidence? I think not. God had given us the privilege of reconnecting them and, moreover, He had given us a huge, thundering affirmation of His direction for us and a reminder of His providential hand.

I could go on about all the ways that God confirmed His plan for us and gave us assurance throughout the process. What a gift! Years later, when our son Erick was a preschooler, he would jump up in the bed with Denise and me at night and lie between us with his little arms folded behind his head and say, "Tell me the story of how *we* got *me*."

Wow! What a wonderful privilege to tell him the story of his adoption complete with all the great grace moments that fill it. God showed Himself and His plan and gave us the gift of stories that help our son know of God's love for Him. Our story, like all adoption stories, is a little illustration of the gospel, complete with signs and movements from God. We are thankful to have our story and to still be experiencing it, but our first adoption also opened my eyes to some hard realities.

THE STARTING BLOCKS

The reality that I came face-to-face with after we came home from Ukraine with Erick was that the hard part of adoption was just beginning. Sure, our social worker had prepared us by having us read a mountain of books and attend a ton of seminars, but I was not fully prepared for how tough the weeks and months were going to be after we returned home.

During the roller-coaster experience of journeying toward adopting a child, I think we actually viewed bringing a child home as the finish line. In reality, that moment was just us coming off the starting blocks. Our son had gotten off to a tough start. As an 18-month-old, he was in the third percentile in height and weighed roughly the same as an average 9-month-old boy. He didn't sit up on his own until he was 11 months old, and he just began to walk before we brought him home to America with us. He was not yet talking, and he had serious developmental delays in almost every facet of life.

Moreover, we went from never having a child to having a walking, solid-food-eating, little bundle of energy who couldn't understand a thing we said to him. Our learning curve was steep, and it still seems steep at times as we try to parent all three of our children well.

From personal experience, I am convinced that if we are going to call upon the church to adopt as a means for living out God's heart for orphans, then we have to do a better job of *equipping* families and *supporting* families as they adopt. And the adoption process is just scratching the surface. The bigger story of global orphan care involves the millions of unadoptable orphans who stand in need of care.

ORPHAN CARE: MORE THAN ADOPTION

While I was overjoyed by our adoption, there was a counterbalance to my joy. I was moved and saddened by the dozens of other children in our son's orphanage that we couldn't adopt and bring home. The memories of those kids struck me in a way that changed me. I will never forget a little boy who was in isolation care in the orphanage in a room next to where our little Erick was recuperating from pneumonia. When we went to visit Erick, that little boy would stand at the door with his caregiver and look longingly at us as we played together. We could tell that he wanted to play, too, but he couldn't join us. He was kept isolated. The thought of what has happened to that little boy has never left me, and God has used it to fuel my passion for the fatherless. According to the

Bible, it is God's plan for that boy and the millions like him to be the responsibility of God's people.

The needs of orphans around the globe are both vast and complex. No one book can hope to deal with all of the intricacies or all of our necessary responses. Instead, we will explore some of the key questions and practices regarding how the church can care for the scores of orphans all over the globe in a way that is consistent with the gospel. But first, we must deal with the question of why we should care for orphans and why our care must extend to the ends of the earth. By answering that question well, we place the global orphan-care and adoption movement on a sure and enduring footing and ensure our efforts bring glory to God.

International Orphan Care and the Gospel: How Do They Fit Together?

I BELIEVE ANY HEALTHY CHRISTIAN MOVEMENT MUST begin with a sound biblical basis. To build a healthy biblical theology about anything, you must start with the Hero of the story, Jesus. So ask yourself when you read the Bible: *What kind of mental picture of Jesus do I come away with? What was He was really like?* As I read the Gospels, I love the way Jesus' personality shows through in the texts, and I think His personality is what is most easily overlooked. At times, it is easier to see a caricature of Jesus that is more reminiscent of the blond, weepy-eyed, frail man that is portrayed in the popular painting of Jesus that has graced the walls of so many grandmothers, rather than as the strong, witty rabbi that the Gospels present.

Think about it. Most of the films about Jesus portray Him as somewhat aloof and disconnected from people, but that's not how the Scriptures present Him at all. He came to live among people and build authentic community with His followers. Instead of being aloof, Jesus came to be fully engaged and present with people. Often, we struggle to see how much He genuinely enjoyed it. Even when He was rebuking someone, Jesus had a witty, even humorous, edge. Take for example the encounter that Jesus had with the scribe in Mark 12:

> *And one of the scribes came up and heard them disputing with one another, and seeing that he answered them well, asked him, "Which command-ment is the most important of all?" Jesus answered, "The most important is, 'Hear, O Israel: The LORD our God, the LORD is one. And you shall love the LORD your God with all your heart and with all your soul and with all your mind and with all your strength.' The second is this: 'You shall love your neighbor as yourself.' There is no other commandment greater than these"* (Mark 12:28–31).

Jesus' wit in this moment really makes me laugh. Picture the scene. Here is this theological legal eagle stepping forward to challenge Jesus with what he perceives is a difficult question (posed to God Himself). It is really absurd, and on some level, the outcome has to be somewhat humorous. The scribe believes his question will blindside Jesus and discredit Him among His disciples. Jesus responded in a way that was both true and funny. Instead of being stumped, Jesus quoted and extended the command to love God supremely from Deuteronomy 6:4–6. It is ironic that as a scribe of Israel, this man was surely wearing a box (phylactery) tied around his forehead that had within it several verses of Scripture including:

> *"Hear, O Israel: The LORD our God, the LORD is one.*
> *You shall love the LORD your God with all your heart*

and with all your soul and with all your might. And
these words that I command you today shall be on
your heart. You shall teach them diligently to your
children, and shall talk of them when you sit in your
house, and when you walk by the way, and when you
lie down, and when you rise. You shall bind them
as a sign on your hand, and they shall be as front-
lets between your eyes. You shall write them on the
doorposts of your house and on your gates"
(Deuteronomy 6:4–9).

Hilarious! Jesus responded in a way that called out the silliness of the question to the scribe and everyone who was listening. This respected teacher of the Law had missed the big *E* on the eye chart. Jesus wryly pointed out that the answer to his own question was literally tied right between His eyes all the time! The little box contained this very section of Scripture from Deuteronomy, and he had missed the link between the truth he wore and the truth Jesus taught. The contents of the box were to serve as a constant reminder that he was to devote his whole heart to God. Moreover, that box was there to remind him that, without the mercy and grace of God, he was hopeless.

We all need to be reminded that we are hopeless. God is holy and just, and we are not. Our unholiness and unjustness had separated us from God, and are the reason God moved to rescue and redeem us. In spite of the fact this religious Hebrew man quoted this Scripture to himself several times a day and had it tied around his forehead, he had missed its meaning. His over-sight is tragic. He was missing out on the transforming love that God had for him. Ultimately, the love that God wants His people to live out is really just a small taste of His love for people. God's love was made perfect in Jesus who was standing right in front of this scribe, but he just didn't see

Because God said so.

it. He didn't see it because he was preoccupied with religious formalities and self-justification. He was missing out on the blessing of redemption and reconciliation that Jesus offered him in salvation, but he also missed out on the blessing that Jesus offered him through the opportunity to live out God's heart by being a blessing to others in His name.

It is easy to criticize the scribe, but I have to admit that I was not too different from him. As I said in chapter 1, I was a guy who had studied theology and taught in seminary, but I had missed truly understanding God's heart for vulnerable people such as orphans, widows, and sojourners. I missed the gospel significance of caring for the voiceless. Over the years, I sat through hundreds of sermons and probably twice as many Bible studies and never heard anyone make the link between the good news that Jesus had come to take away the sins of the world and His church's responsibility to defend the defenseless. To be fair, it was my responsibility to see it, and I hadn't. I had never really grasped God's adopting love for me and my adoption into the family of God through Christ. I imagine that I was not alone in my ignorance, and I am sure that many in the church still don't grasp the glorious truth of our adoption in Christ. I am thankful that God dealt mercifully and even humorously with my ignorance and indifference. I am more thankful that He helped me to see Him in some important places in His Word.

EXTENDING A COVERING

As we consider caring for children or adopting them across national borders, I think God's heart for the sojourner applies to our actions. We are a mechanism for covering them. We are a means to extending some level of grace to them. We are a tangible expression to them of God's care for them and His love for them. This is an underexplored biblical theme, but understanding God's heart for the sojourner can help us understand why it is imperative that we care for orphans all over the world.

Sojourners—strangers in the land of Israel—were easily victimized, and there was nothing they could do about their ethnicity, nothing they could do to remedy their circumstances. They stood in need of a covering of protection, and God mandated that His people should provide that covering. God ordered His people to act in a way that was qualitatively different from the nations around them and to care for these legally helpless outsiders. Why? Every parent can identify with the answer: Because God said so. Because that is God's character and the way He acts. God was unwavering in His command to them never to oppress sojourners. And, when they rebelled against His command, a recommitment to care for the sojourner was always part of their required repentance (e.g., Jeremiah 7:5–7). Why? Because the sojourners within Israel were a living object lesson of who mankind is to God. (We too have no inherent right to be part of His kingdom.) Sojourners were outsiders who were to be treated as insiders in every way.

When we were estranged from Him, He sought us out and provided a covering for us. When we were unable to save ourselves or provide for our own redemption, He provided for us in Jesus. Just as He wanted Israel to live in such a way that they demonstrated His character to the entire world, He wants us to live that way too. Not just because it treats people well (and it does), but because it shows the world who He is. After all, orphan care is about displaying the glory of Christ by defending the defenseless, and most of the defenseless children on the planet live outside of the United States.

WHAT'S SO SPECIAL ABOUT THEM?

Repeatedly throughout the Old Testament narrative, we find a consistent association among widows, orphans, and sojourners. This association is particularly related to God's call for holiness from His people. God associates caring for these three groups as evidence of His people's obedience and righteousness (Deuteronomy 10:18; 14:28–29). God even says abuse of vulnerable groups, such as widows, the fatherless, and the sojourner, sometimes identified as poor or oppressed, is among the most glaring evidence of the disobedience of His people (Isaiah 1:17; 10:2; Jeremiah 5).

The simple questions I would ask are: Why? What is so special about these groups? Why is their plight so close to the heart of God? Why are they different than other types of hurting people and, ultimately, how does care for them illuminate the gospel?

As we seek to answer these questions, we can unlock some essential truths that guide our ministry to the fatherless and can serve as theological guides or boundaries. In particular, the grounding this answer provides can help to serve our decision making about how we care for those in distant lands, who struggle without families.

There really is something special in the biblical association of orphans, widows, and sojourners in God's commands to the nation of Israel. I have come to think of them as theological *running buddies* or a *triad of concern*. Almost every time you see one referenced in the Old Testament, the other two are present. And when they are mentioned together, their mention is always for a specific purpose.

For instance, in Deuteronomy 10:16, God commanded Israel to "circumcise" their hearts. He didn't want them to do surgery on their physical hearts. He wanted them to commit themselves to an ethical standard that would set them apart from the nations around them and reflect His character to those nations. He wanted His people to act differently and show love on His behalf in a way that announces the gospel. He told them to do it because the children of Israel were themselves once sojourners when they lived in Egypt and eventually were enslaved there. God brought them out of Egypt and gave them a land and an identity. They were to be His love in action to vulnerable people to show the salvation that would come in Christ.

In carrying on the work to aid the defenseless, Israel put a couple of important aspects of God's redemptive character on display. First, they gave a tangible illustration of God's love and justice to a sin-sick world that lacks perfect love and justice. They bore witness to God's redemptive plan to restore the world back to its perfect created order, a plan that would be ultimately fulfilled through Jesus. When Israel cared for voiceless victims who had no ability to help themselves, they helped those people, but ultimately they acted in the interests of God. They showed the nations God's character and the way to Him.

They were also giving a taste of the restorative work of the gospel to heal what is broken by sin. Orphans, widows, and sojourners are classes of people whose peril would not exist apart from the fall of man and the entry of sin into the world. In the beginning, God created a perfect world in which women would never lose their husbands because death would not reign; children would not lose parents to death, indifference, substance abuse, poverty, or slavery; and there would be no lines between countries that struggle against each other for a sovereignty that only belongs to God. In righting the wrongs that are done against these most vulnerable victims, God's people shed light on the brokenness of the world and the undeniable need for rescue and restoration that is beyond man to accomplish. The actions of His people in caring for the vulnerable did not and cannot bring ultimate salvation to anyone, but they bring immediate relief of temporal suffering, and they point to a coming eternal kingdom whose King is Jesus.

It's silly to suggest that by righting a few earthly wrongs anyone could satisfy the deficit account that our sin has created with God, but it does testify to the saving work of God found in the gospel. Only redemption through faith in Christ can accomplish salvation, but in committing little acts of earthly redemption, Israel was demonstrating the heart of God and pointing to the coming rescue that would be found in Jesus.

Remember the Lord's Prayer? Jesus taught His closest followers—and us by extension—to pray by asking the Father that His kingdom would come and His will would be done right here on earth. That is the re-creation that Jesus brings by working through the redeemed right here, right now. As we care for widows, orphans, and sojourners, we are righting wrongs and testifying to the healing nature of a faith relationship with God that is made through the acceptance of His Son.

REBUILDING THE ORPHAN-CARE WALL

Stories like mine are becoming commonplace as evangelicals rediscover orphan care. What is happening reminds me a great deal of Israel's recovery of the Law in Nehemiah 8. The city was in shambles as a result of the desertion and inattention of the exile years. The Law of God had been lost to the people. In rebuilding the city, the people rediscovered the Law, but, more importantly, they reconnected with the heart of God. In similar fashion, the church today has recovered a passion for orphan care by a return to deep biblical exposition.

Until a few years ago, the conversation regarding God's heart for the orphan and the modern evangelical church's role in caring for orphans was almost completely nonexistent. While the evangelical church had a rich history of caring for the fatherless in our distant past, a seismic shift took place somewhere along the way. Ministry to the fatherless, like much of our ministry to the "least of these," ground to a halt. There were certainly pockets of concern but, as a general rule, conservative Bible-believing churches abdicated their role in orphan care and most other forms of mercy ministry.

What a difference a few years makes! Today, the biblical and theological foundations for Christians' care for the fatherless and for adoption are well documented. Christian pastors and theologians such as Tom Davis, John Piper, Russ Moore, Dan Cruver, Tony Merida, and so many others have challenged the church to engage in orphan care and adoption in light of the gospel. Further, they have helped us to understand the gospel not just as the story of Jesus' birth, life, death, resurrection, and return. They have helped us identify that the gospel is the full story of God's redemptive work over all of the Scriptures. To keep

41

a proper perspective on orphan care, we have to keep the whole gospel before us.

TO THE UTTERMOST PARTS

The gospel demands we be engaged in orphan care and adoption internationally. To that end, when we care for orphans who live beyond our country's borders, we are really trampling down the results of the fall and testifying to the gospel. We are acknowledging that the gospel of Jesus knows no borders and no prejudice. Everyone has the opportunity to receive the grace that Jesus extended—no matter where they are born and no matter the conditions of their birth.

I believe there are similar reasons for adopting internationally and caring for orphans around the globe. When we adopt internationally and care for orphans without regard for national boundaries, we deny the arbitrary distinctions that human beings have made to separate ourselves from one another by drawing borders and defending them. Ultimately, differences in country and language are a result of the fall; and when we go beyond them in orphan care and adoption, we are testifying to the triumph of the gospel to shatter those distinctions.

Further, when we adopt transracially, with no regard for skin color or ethnicity, we are affirming that all are created in the image of God and that in Christ there is neither Greek nor Jew. Transracial adoptive families are lovely pictures (in black-and-white or color) of the fact that there are no distinctions in God's family. In a spiritual sense, this colorblindness and disregard of geographic distinctions is a true parallel of our coming to Christ, and our care for orphans internationally is a key to driving this truth home to a world that is dying to hear it. I am thankful that

God has granted us such ways to display the gospel, and I pray that we will walk wisely in those ways.

This is not to say that we want to be imperialistic bullies in the name of this gospel either. Jesus always calls upon His followers to act in ways that are legally responsible and socially sensitive. Jesus respected the laws and customs of His day—when they were not standing between people and their worship of God. We should too. I don't think anyone of any credibility in the evangelical orphan-care and adoption movement wants to do anything other than to honor God and to do what is best for the most vulnerable children among us.

In fact, sometimes our failures point to God and His gospel as well as our successes do. Sometimes we have a tendency to overromanticize the connection between spiritual and earthly adoption. I think we can get in real danger when we talk about spiritual and earthly adoptions interchangeably without drawing broad distinctions in our rhetoric and pointing out the gross differences as well as the similarities. Bluntly, we are not God. He is a perfect parent, and none of us is. Sometimes we testify to the glory of God in adoption as much by how far short we fall as parents from His ideal as we do by any resemblance to His adopting grace. Object lessons can be helpful in giving a point of reference to understand deep, abstract things about God, but, in the end, those object lessons always fall short of fully encompassing the greater spiritual reality they represent. The theology of adoption is no exception. God's adoption of us is the definition of adoption, and our adoption of children is an illustration of that definition, not the equivalent of God's redemptive work. Earthly adoption (and orphan care) points to God, but it falls pitifully short. Earthly adoption is merely a taste of the unlimited banquet of grace found in God's adopting character.

Further, we are struggling to explain orphan care and adoption in ways that make sense to the world outside the church. While our internal dialogue in the church regarding God's plan for the world uses terms such as *rescue* and *redemption*, the rest of the world is talking about *empowerment* and *opportunity*. As my friend Chris Marlow of Help One Now said to me,

> I think that's part of where the adoption conversation struggles for the world outside the church. They aren't thinking about adoption theologically. They aren't thinking, *I want to go over there and rescue that kid*. They are thinking, *I want to go over there to help them become future leaders*. How does the church say, "Adoption is necessary"; but at the same time, how does the church say, "Go empower local leaders"?

We must consider how to winsomely advance this discussion among our friends and our detractors to keep the focus on the gospel. We must think more deeply about how we talk about orphan care and adoption so that we share the gospel winsomely with those in the world outside the church rather than alienate them.

Wrestling to know God through His Word will inevitably bring us face-to-face with Him. We cannot ever encounter God and walk away unchanged. Ultimately, good theology in the hands of true disciples will always lead to ministry. Discovering the deep connection between His heart for orphans and the gospel in God's Word challenges us to mobilize the church to act. Passivity or intellectual assent to the plight of orphans will not satisfy God, and it cannot satisfy us. We must find practical ways to bring our theology into action.

How Do We Mobilize the Church to Engage Orphans Worldwide?

I HAVE HEARD THE AMERICAN CHURCH REFERRED to in many sermons as a "sleeping giant." When I think of the potential of the church in the United States to impact the world with the gospel through orphan care, I cannot help but think this is an appropriate moniker. America is responsible for almost 19 percent of the world's gross domestic product (GDP), and its citizens are the seventh richest people in the world. We have the means to impact the world's orphan crisis, but America's potential isn't merely economic. According to Fraser Institute's World Freedom Index, America is the seventh freest country on earth. While evangelicals might quibble with the Fraser Institute's definition of freedom, this index underscores the fairly unfettered opportunity of Americans to go and do in the name of Jesus without legal constraint or persecution.

Bluntly, we have the means, the opportunity, and the call from God to ease the suffering of orphaned and vulnerable children around the world in Jesus' name. There is nothing preventing us from accomplishing significant things to aid orphans in ways that point to Jesus' sacrifice for the world, and there has never been a better time than now. The globe has never been more accessible through travel and technology. Moreover, God seems to be doing something special on behalf of the fatherless and the vulnerable, and where He is at work, we need to join Him. Passivity from the church does not honor God, and it will not result in the kind of worldwide activity that is needed to help orphans. We have to wake the sleeping giant. We have to mobilize the church to care for the world's orphans. The question is, *How?*

PERSISTENCE IN PRAYER

I have lost count of the number of times I have had what amounts to the same conversation with different people in different places. It usually begins something like this: They walk up after a sermon or presentation and say, "I read *Orphanology* and loved it, but we are really struggling to get an orphan ministry off the ground in our church. There are a few of us that are passionate about orphan care, but we can't seem to get our pastor to catch the vision."

I ask them a couple of simple questions. The first is, "How have you engaged your pastor?" Their answers usually involve meetings, emails, giving him videos, and so on. The common theme of the answers is that they have either spent a great deal of time and energy trying to make a case to convince the pastor, or they have tried to emotionally engage him. That leads me to my second question, "How much have you been praying for your pastor?" That question is most often met with an uncomfortable, rather embarrassed stare.

Unwittingly, these very well-intentioned people have become more of a *Martha* in their passionate pursuit of their orphan-care goal than a *Mary* (Luke 10:38–42). Often, these folks are really discouraged and defeated, but they shouldn't be. Remember,

"The king's heart is a stream of water in the hand of the LORD; he turns it wherever he will" (Proverbs 21:1). The pastor's heart is no different, and I know because I was that pastor. I had a wife who prayed persistently for me like the persistent widow (Luke 18:1–7).

If you want your pastor and your church to "get it" with regard to orphan care, be willing to labor in prayer and forget about becoming a clanging cymbal. All that your nagging will get you are church leaders who will turn and go the other way when they see you coming. Seek out other people who are passionate about caring for orphans and pray together a lot. Pray that God will give the people in your church a vision for the gospel and the nations. Pray that God will make His name famous by defending the defenseless through your church. Pray that God will guide your steps to the place(s) He has set aside for you to serve. As you pray, God will honor your faithfulness and trust in Him with more faithfulness and provision than you can imagine. Perhaps that provision will come in a blessing of your plans. Perhaps it will come in God leading your church leadership to engage orphans differently. However it comes, God is for orphans and He will honor your consistent petition.

TEACH THE BIBLE DIFFERENTLY

Another reason that Christians aren't passionate about orphan care is they haven't seen God's heart for the orphan in the Scriptures. They don't know how important orphan care is to displaying God's character to people or telling the gospel to the world. To change that, we have to teach the Bible differently. For far too long in too many churches, we have approached Bible study as if the Bible were written to fix our problems. It wasn't.

The Bible was written to reveal God and His story of redemption for His glory. The real miracle is seen when we view it as it was intended (although the Bible certainly has practical value for our hurts and problems too). When we play hopscotch all over the Bible, jumping from book to book and story to story with no overarching reason, we miss the larger threads of meaning that develop through the storyline. Threads like:

• How God is telling the world who He is
• What He is doing for it through Jesus
• How He asks His people to care for orphans throughout history

We need to teach people that storyline in chronology and in context to help them see the intention of God in history and to show them how to live with purpose every day. The great news is that a ton of curriculum tools have been produced in the last several years to help churches teach this way through small groups and Sunday School. Look for Bible studies that teach the storyline of Scripture and focus on teaching the big themes that come out of the story in terms of the gospel. When people see the Bible that way, orphan care just becomes logical and natural, rather than being a forced aspect of church programming.

BEGIN SIMPLY

If your church is not engaged in orphan care at all, the likelihood that you will begin at the point of a full-scale, comprehensive ministry to orphans is low. More likely is that you will start small, get on your feet with a few baby steps, and then in time be able to step out with a full strategy for orphan care that mobilizes your church.

So where do you begin? Most churches have a few likely places to start. If there is openness on the part of your church leadership, participating in

Our hope is that our support will help.

Orphan Sunday on the first Sunday in November is a good way to raise awareness and stir the conversation in your congregation about gospel-centered orphan care. Facilitated by the Christian Alliance for Orphans, the Orphan Sunday website (orphansunday .org) provides a variety of resources videos, sermon notes, small-group lessons, children and youth ministry ideas, prayer guides, bulletin inserts, and more. If Orphan Sunday is still a bit much for your church, perhaps you could suggest including an emphasis on orphans as part of another emphasis day, such as Sanctity of Human Life Sunday or World Hunger Sunday. While these days are not specifically set aside to focus on the plight of orphans, the global orphan crisis is a relevant component of each of the issues upon which these days are focused. Perhaps you could host an information session after church or insert information about the global orphan crisis in your church's bulletin as part of the church's overall emphasis on one of these days.

WALK BEFORE YOU RUN

Taking things a step further, maybe your church would host a Compassion Sunday for Compassion International (compassion .com). I would consider Compassion an orphan-prevention ministry that provides for vulnerable children through child sponsorships. Compassion's commitment to Christ, children, the church, and their integrity has always impressed me. Having met dozens of the ministry's graduates over the years, I am always inspired by the stories of how Compassion impacts young people with the gospel. Compassion places great emphasis on discipling them, educating them, and supporting their families through the local church.

Our family has been involved with Compassion personally for several years through sponsoring a child. For just a few dollars per month, our family has had the privilege of helping Compassion accomplish their mission: "In response to the Great Commission, Compassion International exists as an advocate for children, to release them from their spiritual, economic, social, and physical poverty and enable them to become responsible and fulfilled Christian adults." We have also formed a special relationship with a child in South America with whom we correspond and for whom we pray regularly. Our hope is that our support will help to keep his family intact, keep him healthy, provide for his education, and give him the opportunity to contribute to building God's kingdom and his nation as an adult leader.

In April of each year, churches all over host a Compassion Sunday to give church members an easy, low-pressure opportunity to sponsor a child through Compassion International. The plan is simple. Someone gives a brief testimony about Compassion in the church's worship service and a brief video is shown. In addition, a table is set up in a visible location displaying sponsorship cards for children who are awaiting sponsorship. Something like Compassion Sunday is a great way to raise awareness of the plight of vulnerable children around the globe and to give a large number of people a way to become personally invested in it with gospel purpose. Once you have broken the ice with involvement, you may find that subsequent conversations about more involvement to help orphans will become easier.

ENTRY-LEVEL OPPORTUNITIES
FOR THE WHOLE CHURCH

Every Christian shouldn't adopt a child (for various reasons) nor is every Christian going to have a deep, life-altering engagement in orphan care. Because of this, we need to give them entry-level opportunities to get involved. Many churches find that establishing an adoption fund is a great way to involve a broad cross-section of the congregation in ministering to orphans. Adoptions (especially transnational adoptions) can be quite expensive, and establishing an adoption fund can help families afford to adopt by offering grants or zero-interest loans. There are two major issues in church adoption funds: establishing and managing the fund and raising the money for the fund.

Adoption funds are a great idea in theory, but they can be difficult for churches to manage. It is a good idea to engage a ministry partner like Lifesong for Orphans to help with managing the church's adoption fund. Lifesong lifts the burden for managing the fund from church leadership by screening applicants according to criteria established by the church and maximizing stewardship by ensuring compliance to all IRS procedures. Best of all, Lifesong provides its adoption fund management services at no cost to churches. To date, Lifesong manages more than 250 church funds and has participated in funding more than 3,200 adoptions.

Many churches demonstrate great creativity in raising the money to establish adoption funds. Here are a few ideas to spur your thinking. One idea might be to take up a special offering on Father's Day with the proceeds going to fund adoptions. This year, our church is hosting a 5K fun run on the weekend of Orphan Sunday for the entire community to raise funds and awareness. Another idea might be to sell T-shirts, which are another way to raise awareness. They prompt people to ask questions, and they can prompt those who know their meaning to pray. Fund the Nations is an innovative ministry that has taken the hassle out of raising funds for missional causes by selling T-shirts. (They also work directly with adopting families who are raising funds.) The Fund the Nations process is easy and reduces the financial burden on the church/family funds. Here's how the process works:

- You contact Fund the Nations through fundthenations.com with information about why you're raising money.
- They work with you to create a design related to your orphan (or other) ministry that will fit your community's interests and style.
- You presell T-shirts via Facebook, Twitter, email, or other social media.
- When you're finished collecting orders and money, you email Fund the Nations the sizes you need.
- They print and ship them to you for distribution.

Fund the Nations has provided a fund-raising model that requires no money upfront and gives assurance that you won't get stuck with shirts you don't need or can't sell. Fund the Nations has already seen God do some amazing things for His kingdom through T-shirts. They have helped people raise money to go on missions trips to more than 150 different countries, states, and cities and raised more than $250,000 per year for adoptions and the spread of the gospel.

RUN FOR THE PRIZE

Some churches are far past the beginning stages of establishing an orphan ministry. But there really is no template or preferred strategy for how to do it. The styles and forms churches have used are as varied as the communities of which they are a part. Some churches have gone all in on their global orphan-care strategy. One such church is Long Hollow Baptist Church in Hendersonville, Tennessee. In 2009, God began to stir up the leadership at Long Hollow to do something to respond to James 1:27 and care for orphans. I can't possibly tell you all that God is doing in and through their church in adoption and orphan care here, but let me tell you one story to illustrate.

Long Hollow Baptist wanted to do something to care for orphans among the nations. As they researched, they were captivated by the plight of orphans in Haiti in particular. In conjunction with the Global Orphan Project, some Long Hollow members led by executive pastor Lance Taylor took a vision trip to Haiti to explore finding a partner to do orphan ministry. God led them to the western coastal town of Jeremie and El Shaddai Ministries International (ESMI) to form a partnership. The contours of this partnership were certainly flexible but nonetheless well defined. ESMI, under the leadership of Dr. Domy St. Germain, was interested in establishing a church and a children's village and school to care for local orphans. Long Hollow would raise the funds to build the village, provide construction teams, medical teams, discipleship support, and any logistical support needed by the local leaders. In the beginning, this partnership was achieved with the Global Orphan Project offering consultation and support, but eventually it became a direct partnership involving only Long Hollow and the local Haitian congregation. Ultimately, the goal of the project is the empowerment of the local leaders in creating a self-sufficient Haitian children's village. Little did they know, God would be putting them on the ground in advance of the January 2010 earthquake with an opportunity to help quickly.

Before the earthquake happened, God had led Long Hollow into an ambitious Crazy Love Campaign to seek to raise $3.5 million in a series of five offerings over the course of 2009 and 2010. Through a portion of those offerings, they were able to fund the construction costs for the children's village. Additionally, they began seeking sponsorships to cover the cost of schooling, a hot meal, and a daily snack at $45 per month. They asked sponsors to commit to a three-year term to allow the village to reach self-sufficiency. The offerings and the sponsorships gave a large number of Long Hollow members a way to be personally involved in orphan care.

Because Long Hollow was already engaged in Haiti with a flexible partnership in which the locals were significantly invested in crafting the strategy, when the earthquake hit adjustments to the plan were made. First, they absorbed a small orphanage in Port-au-Prince into their midst. Second, they expanded their school to accommodate children from the surrounding community. The results have had a great impact in many lives, and those results were a direct result of empowering local leaders appropriately.

According to Erica Ho, Long Hollow's mission specialist responsible for coordinating the church's Love a L.O.T. (Least of These) orphan ministry, the church worked with certain under-lying convictions in establishing the partnership. For instance, they have wanted the Haitian people to accept that the children's village and medical services are the work of the local church and the anchor point of the village. "We always refer to ourselves as visitors who are here at the invitation of the local church," Erica said.

The church sends 16 missions teams per year to work at the children's village in Jeremie. Medical teams go twice per year to give checkups to all the children and supplement the care of the staff doctor and nurse. Those teams also see patients from the surrounding community. "People in Jeremie don't have access to doctors, and our teams will see 900 patients on a trip," Erica said. These trips connect the local church and the children's home to the community. The trips also connect Long Hollow members to the children in the children's village. A significant number of the people who travel to Haiti each year are returnees, and some even go multiple times each year.

Another conviction is that Long Hollow members do not bring gifts to the children except for during an annual Christmas trip. All gifts and provisions are given through their Haitian pastors and caregivers. I love that Long Hollow goes to great lengths to put the spotlight on their local church partner to add to that church's credibility. Ultimately, Long Hollow's goal is to advance the gospel, not to win praise for their ministry.

I hope you will not be overwhelmed by the scope of the ministry in this example and shrug it off as too far out of reach for you. What Long Hollow has done is certainly scaled to the size of their church, but the convictions behind its outreach will fit any church of any size.

DON'T REINVENT THE WHEEL

Most churches already have some sort of mission strategy or at least some missions activity. Instead of trying to run off in a completely different direction, why not look for opportunities to take what your church is already invested in and leverage it for orphan care? My favorite illustration of doing this is one that we shared in *Orphanology*, but it is the best example I know. Our preschool choir leaders wanted to get preschoolers involved in orphan care, so they began collecting new shoes to give to orphans. The response was overwhelming. We had more shoes than we knew what to do with, and the choir leaders said to us pastors, "OK, we have all these shoes, now you guys figure out what to do with them."

Wow! Thanks! So we prayed, and God answered. Here is what we felt led to do. Instead of building another program, we decided it made sense to find a ministry to orphans and vulnerable children in the places we were already engaged at home, nationally, and globally. So, that's what we did. Every missions team we sent out took shoes to a partner where we were already engaged. Over time, those shoes were a vehicle to establish and strengthen ties between our ministry partners and orphan ministries in their own areas. Many of our ministry partners had struggled to connect with these orphan ministries previously. Sometimes, God uses the simplest ideas to bring about significant fruit.

CROCK-POTS, NOT MICROWAVES

We live in a society that expects instant results. Think about the last time you were at your favorite fast-food restaurant and the cashier told you that it would be two minutes until your french fries would be ready. You may not admit it, but I will. My first thought is, *Oh great, like I have time to stand here and wait!* Seriously, who do I think I am? Of course I have a couple of minutes to wait on fries, but I have become conditioned to not having to wait for anything—to expect instant gratification. The tendency to want results immediately really isn't helpful or realistic in orphan ministry.

We need churches to strategize with long-term goals in mind. Look for global partners in whom you can make consistent, enduring investments of resources and presence. One big reason is the kids to whom you will be ministering. Orphans have been let down by significant people in their lives. Some of them have been let down by *lots* of significant people, and they need stability and consistency, not people who are going to run in for a *feel-good* opportunity. Without trying to be too harsh or hypercritical, I want to be direct. Orphan ministry is not about us. If you need to feel good, go and volunteer at an animal shelter (the animals will be glad to see you and won't hold it against you if they never see you again), but keep your distance from orphans. They need people who will come back. Let me be clear. I am not against short-term missions trips, but I am against short-term missions trips that do not advance long-term goals. If you are not working with a partner that is including you as part of a long-term plan or if your church does not have a long-term plan for involvement with orphans in a place where you establish work, then please find some other way to be involved from a distance.

CONSUME WITH A PURPOSE

With all the recent emphasis on Christians living humbly and radically, many folks are a little awash in a sea of confusion. I think it is healthy for us all to evaluate how we are living and to examine if the decisions, big and small, in our lives are being made with building Christ's kingdom in mind. For a few people that could result in a rather radical shift in life—like selling everything and moving to Ethiopia to care for orphans. But for most of us, it will be more like a radical shift in how we think and act in our day-to-day lives. One of the ways that we can make a subtle but significant shift is what I would call purposeful consuming: buying products that we would buy anyway from sources that support healthy ministries and causes. Let me give you an example. Almost all of us give Christmas and birthday gifts to friends and family. What if those gifts could make a greater difference? Established in 1996, WorldCrafts℠ develops sustainable, fair-trade businesses among impoverished people around the world. Its vision is simple but ambitious: offer an income with dignity and the hope of everlasting life to every person on earth. To accomplish this vision, WorldCrafts partners with dozens of artisan groups in dozens of nations of the world to import and sell hundreds of fine, handcrafted items.

By investing in product development, maintaining certain levels of product orders, and encouraging sustainable production practices, people who purchase items from WorldCrafts help create viable employment for women and men in poverty. Women no longer need to turn to prostitution for their next meal. Parents can provide education and nutrition to their children. Men can use their artisanal skills to earn a fair and reliable income without leaving their families, and the gifts that you give for Christmas and birthdays can take on an eternal significance.

Many WorldCrafts artisan groups are working to free women involved in human trafficking and sexual exploitation. You can read the stories of each artisan group and learn how your shopping and gift giving through WorldCrafts can help orphans (and sometime prevent the creation of more orphans) at WorldCrafts.org.

LET A HAND BE A HAND

In 1 Corinthians 12, Paul uses a silly illustration to make a clear point to the church about the use of gifts. He points out the absurdity of people ranking their importance in the church because of their gifting by saying it would be like a person's foot wanting to leave the body because it doesn't get to be a hand. We understand the ridiculousness of Paul's illustration, yet I think we sometimes struggle to actually apply it in the church. Missions enterprises like orphan ministry can be a perfect example. Instead of matching the natural gifting and ability of people to the needs of the place we are ministering, we try to mold people to fit the tasks that we think need to be done. What results is often wasted time and wasted talent. Let me illustrate with a personal mistake.

Several years ago, I took a friend who is an entrepreneurial businessman on a missions trip with me. Let's call him Jim. Our team was going to help a church planter in Eastern Europe with a church launch. We were there strategically to be a catalyst to him engaging a Roma community through medical clinics and some sports clinics. All in all, we had a good plan, but I really missed it with Jim. He was great where we placed him working with the sports camps, but he could do that in his sleep. Every time Jim got close to our young church planter host, he peppered this young pastor with questions. I was fascinated. I spent a great deal of time just watching and listening to the two of them.

A few days after we got home, Jim came by my office. He was fired up. He had a ream of papers in his hand. They were emails that he had already exchanged with our church planter friend.

Jim waved those printed emails at me with a look of genuine excitement and said,

> "That dude needs to find a way to make a living. He needs a way to support himself so he can feed his family and get his church off the ground, and there are tons more just like him. I am working with him to put a business plan together, and I am getting some guys together to talk about how to build a network to get them start-up money!"

What has grown out of Jim's gift for seeing a need that he was gifted to help meet is an indigenous program that helps church planters form business plans and then provides them with no-interest microloans to get them started. I tell this story to make a point. Often, as we seek to build God's kingdom, we are guilty of underutilizing some of the greatest resources that He has blessed us with: His talented people. We ask gifted people to lay down what they do best to get on our agenda. So, we have a doctor help roof a group home for orphans in Haiti or send the CEO of a multimillion dollar corporation to haul dirt in a wheelbarrow for a week on a construction project. Is that really leveraging their gifts, talents, and abilities in the best way according to 1 Corinthians 12?

What if we looked for international partners with which to invest the know-how and strengths of our people? What if we invested in empowering young leaders (especially orphans) for their future instead of just investing money and tangible resources in their daily lives? I think we could go a long way to ending the cycle of poverty and hopelessness that produces orphans. Why do we want to do that? Because it earns us the right to tell them why we are doing what we are doing: the King of kings and Lord of lords has changed us, and we live for Him.

PREPARING FOR ORPHAN CARE AND ADOPTION

We need to prepare people to do the necessary tasks to accomplish good orphan care and adoption. After all, we teach people skills in the church, such as sharing their faith or managing their finances to the glory of God. Why shouldn't we teach orphan care-related skills? You could train volunteers to address special needs or conditions in your church's preschool, children, and student programming so that they will be ready to accommodate the needs of some adoptive families. You could train people as ESL (English as a second language) teachers and tutors to assist adoptive families and orphan ministry partners. You could teach preadoption classes to give families an opportunity to explore whether adoption is really for them. You could offer support groups for adoptive families who each deal with similar issues and can benefit from both the understanding community and the information sharing that these groups provide.

ENGAGE HUMAN TRAFFICKING
AND CHILD VICTIMIZATION

Another way to become influential in the global orphan crisis is through advocacy training by organizations such as International Justice Mission (IJM). Such organizations can teach you how to engage with government and business leaders to be a voice for the voiceless widows and orphans of the world. You don't have to be a politician or a captain of industry to be able to make a difference. Every voice counts. Opportunities abound for ordinary citizens who are willing to get involved, to hold the need for justice up to elected officials and others.

It is the power of the masses that makes a difference. When we change whom we will vote to support or what we will buy to uphold justice, leaders will listen. Too often, Christians are labeled for what we oppose. Isn't it about time we become heard for what we support—justice for the voiceless and defenseless?

The International Justice Mission is also mobilizing the church in a concerted prayer effort to bring justice to the world in Jesus' name. At the Global Prayer Gathering held each April, people come together to pray, celebrate what God is doing in bringing freedom to the oppressed, and to hear stories of how God is at work rescuing and restoring victims of injustice.

A FEW GOOD MEN

Recently, I had a conversation that really struck me. The talk was with NFL wide receiver David Nelson and his brother Patrick. They, along with their brother Daniel, are the cofounders of I'm ME. The organization I'm ME exists:

> "(1) to raise up the next generation of orphans to know their identity is found in Jesus Christ, each created with their own unique purpose; and (2) to empower, love, and care for each orphan, as well as provide every child with a family environment, education, food, and clean water."

I love these young guys, their story, and their passion for Christ. Our conversation that day tapped into a burden that God has given them to see men engage in orphan care. I'm not sure anyone really knows why there are more women than men involved, but it is imperative that we find ways to get men more involved. These children need healthy male influences and role models. Orphans, particularly those living in institutions, live in environments that are often devoid of male influence. The boys need men to pattern their lives after. The girls need men to show them appropriate love and respect. I don't have the answer to the problem, but we must find an answer. We must find men and get them in the game.

Mobilizing the church to respond to God's call to care for orphans all over the globe means employing a great deal of creativity and flexibility. What is appropriate for one church will not work in the next. All of these ideas are meant merely to spur you on to what God is laying out before you and your church. I hope some of these ideas will inspire your thinking. Above all else, take a step. Follow God's command to care for orphans to the ends of the earth and to put His gospel on display.

Chapter 4

Who Are the World's Orphans Really?

WHEN I WAS GROWING UP, MY FATHER WAS QUITE a handy guy. In fact, I think he could build anything out of wood. Some of his woodworking projects are among my most prized possessions. His work is beautiful and, especially since He went home to be with the Lord, I have really treasured those pieces. I have spent countless hours looking at the intricate workmanship. I can see how hard he worked to get the joints just right or how careful he was to make sure the finish on a piece of stained wood was perfect.

My father was a planner. Before he set out to do a woodworking project, he would plan every detail so carefully that, I have to admit, it drove me crazy. As much as I regret it now, I never learned much of what my father could have taught me because I lacked the patience to stay through all the planning. I wish now I had stayed and learned. Over the years, experience has taught me the value of being a better planner, though I will likely never be the planner my father was.

Planning is certainly involved once we understand that we are all called to "visit" orphans in their distress. To do that we must try to identify who it is that we are going to help and where they are so that we can make a plan as to how best to help them.

We have to *know orphans* if we are ever to move toward a world with *no orphans*!

HOW MANY ARE THERE?

A significant question that comes up with many people when I am talking with them

There are millions of children who are in desperate need of our help, but we need to be careful to use statistics and illustrations with the greatest degree of integrity.

about international orphan care is, "Just exactly how many orphans are there around the world?" Anyone reading this book who is already engaged in global orphan care knows that getting a single, accurate answer to this question is nearly impossible, but remember, our objective isn't just to gather correct statistics. It is to get information that aids our helping orphans. Although numbers aren't always what they seem on the surface, according to the current best estimates, here is what we can be reasonably confident of regarding the world's orphan population: The statistic most often quoted by both those inside and outside the orphan-care community at this time is that there are 153 million orphans worldwide. This number can be misleading. This figure (confirmed by both UNICEF and the United States government) includes both single and double orphans. *Single orphan* is a term to describe a child who has lost one parent to death. *Double orphan* describes a child who has lost both parents to death. The number of double orphans in the world according to these same sources is somewhere under 18 million children.

A glaring difficulty with relying on the UNICEF statistics or in using them to minimize the global orphan crisis is that the number of orphans reported by UNICEF represents children who are *living in homes*! While many of these children meet the biblical definition of the kinds of vulnerable children that the Bible calls orphans or fatherless, we can assume that some percentage of them do not. In the end, the UNICEF number really doesn't help us understand the scope of the problem with any degree of accuracy. We also have to be careful how we use the 153 million orphan statistic.

So, let me be clear. We don't need to give anyone the notion that there are 153 million orphaned children living around the world tonight in need of families as a casual glance at this number would imply. I am afraid that if we use that number, we risk engaging in unhelpful, hyperbolic rhetoric. In the past, I admit that I have been guilty of this oversimplification and, publicly, I want to repent of that error.

Let me also be clear that to not use the UNICEF statistic is *not* to imply that there isn't a huge crisis nor is it to assert that there is anything nefarious in UNICEF's number. UNICEF is a political organization that made a strategic decision to count vulnerable children based upon the death of a parent and primarily related to how losing even one parent affects them. This was done mainly in response to the global AIDS crisis of the mid-1990s.

Simply put, UNICEF and the church have different definitional bases and objectives. In the end, this is more significant than a squabble over statistics. There are millions of children who are in desperate need of our help, but we need to be careful to use statistics and illustrations with the greatest degree of integrity. Some percentage of children who are counted in the 153 million are *not* in need of our help, and acknowledging that fact should be a point of integrity for us.

VULNERABLE CHILDREN

Let's think about it like this: In my church (and I suspect in yours), there are children who live in single-parent families because of the death of one of their parents. The living mothers or fathers in those single-parent families would probably not welcome the idea that, when we talk about the 153 million orphans worldwide, we are counting *their* children. On the other hand, there are many of these children who meet the biblical concept of an orphan. Orphans in the Bible were considered so because they didn't have a father to give them an identity for society to recognize. Still others fall somewhere in between. Right now, these children are part of single-parent families that are in peril of breaking apart as a result of poverty, disease, or victimization by those who would exploit their vulnerability. They need our help too. We need a better, multifaceted definition that takes into account all these statuses of vulnerability.

One number that would be helpful to us would be a comprehensive count of children who stand in need of families, either through adoption or nonkinship foster care. This number would include double orphans who are living outside of the care of extended family, orphaned children who have been abandoned by both their living parents and extended family, and orphaned children who have been permanently removed from the care of their birth parents by government action for reasons of gross neglect and/or abuse. To my knowledge, no single current estimates of the worldwide orphan population addresses how many children fit into each of these life circumstances. This statistic would give us a better understanding from nation to nation of the true picture of the challenge and how the challenge can best be met through a solution of in-country adoptions, foster care, appropriate institutional care, and transnational adoptions.

We also need to have a better handle on how many vulnerable children there are in each nation and better ways of describing their statuses. Most of these children aren't orphans in the sense that many think (alone with no parents), but they have needs that God would have us meet in Jesus' name. Because of their family circumstances, they are in peril of becoming double orphans or abandoned. They need our help. I believe our responsibility here is orphan prevention.

REUNIFICATION

Perhaps one of the greatest challenges in ending the orphan crisis is in seeking the reunification of families. If the UNICEF orphan statistics only count children living in homes, then they do not count the estimated 8 to 10 million orphaned children living in institutions worldwide. Again, not all of these children are adoptable, nor are they all in need of adoption. In fact, personal experience leads me to believe that the majority of institutionalized children in some parts of the world, such as Eastern Europe, are there as a result of family disruption that has the potential to be resolved.

I have witnessed firsthand children growing up in orphanages who are there because their families can't afford to keep them at home or cannot keep them at home because of some significant physical or mental illness or addiction. These kids need our help, but they don't need adoption. Their families need help to find economic stability, a community of support, or some other type of healing in order that these children might go home to a healthy family. The call to care for orphans is a call to be active in this ministry too.

This point hits particularly close to home for me. During the Great Depression, my father was raised by his mother in a single-parent home. Because her husband had died, my grandmother worked a nominal job as the receptionist for a local doctor to provide for her family. In the worst of the fallout from the Depression, she couldn't make enough money to feed all four of her kids and keep a roof over their heads. My dad and his older brother were old enough to take some responsibility for taking care of themselves; they could work shining shoes or selling papers to help out. His youngest brother and sister were too young to work and too young to stay home by themselves while the rest of the family worked. My grandmother made the gut-wrenching decision to place my uncle and aunt (her two youngest children) in an orphanage. Her decision was temporary, and as soon as she was minimally able to provide for her children at home, she removed them from the orphanage and brought them home.

My uncle and aunt weren't really orphans. They weren't adoptable, but they were vulnerable children because they were part of a vulnerable family. They needed support from the body of Christ. They got it in a way that was socially acceptable in that day, but it was help given in a way that most Americans would reject today. Unfortunately, these are the types of social and economic safety nets that still exist as the only alternative in many second- and third-world countries.

Most American Christians would be appalled if the story that I shared about my family had resulted in my aunt and uncle being taken from my grandmother and placed for adoption only because she could not provide for them economically. We would agree that the appropriate answer to caring for them was to offer support to a widow in need and to give her the opportunity to love and nurture her children again as soon as she was able. We would agree that this was providing justice according to the pattern of Isaiah 1:17: "Learn to do good; seek justice, correct oppression; bring justice to the fatherless, plead the widow's cause." That is what the church did for her then, and it is what we should do now in all four corners of the globe.

Sadly, we can point to cases around the world today where families place their children for adoption only because they cannot provide for them. I want to declare without equivocation that poverty alone should not be reason for a birth parent to have to relinquish his or her children for adoption. In the name of Jesus, we should help these families stay together. In our zeal to live out the implications of the gospel through adoption, we have to care for orphans and other vulnerable children appropriately, based upon their status and circumstances.

Reunification strategies call for us to engage at a much deeper level in the lives of people. This will lead us to consider work in areas like economic development, disease prevention, and so on. I know this will lead to the inevitable talks of sacrificing great things for the good in the minds of some because they do not see direct evangelism in our everyday contact with people. For some it will smack of majoring on dealing with temporal suffering instead of dealing with spiritual need. To this oft-argued, seeming conflict, I say that if our efforts to help do not point people to the gospel, then shame on us. If we can't be about the work of reconciliation in families and engaged in the ministry of reconciliation between people and God at the same time, then we should just quit.

My family was exactly the kind of family that needed someone to visit them in their affliction, and the church did. My grandmother worked as hard as she could to pull the ends together and she couldn't. They needed help *and* the gospel!

Looking back, if it hadn't been for a Roman Catholic orphanage in Mobile, Alabama, which stood in the gap for my family, they probably wouldn't have made it.

The orphanage that was used then to help support part of my family was one that would appall us today. My grandmother wasn't allowed to see her two youngest children for months while they were voluntarily "committed" to the orphanage. She used to change the way she walked to work just to catch a glimpse of my aunt who was barely in grade school. I can't imagine the pain, but, in the end, it saved them all.

Critics, who lob stones from outside the Christian orphan-care and adoption movement, point to situations like these as evidence that the movement has always been broken. I point to this time in my family's life to say that notion is rubbish. It saved my family. Sure, we know more today. Our methods need to continue to adapt and evolve, but our long-term history is strong. We need to build upon this heritage to tackle current vexing and complex problems—both the orphan crisis and the needs of vulnerable children and their families.

CHILDREN ON THE STREET

None of the widely used numerical estimates of orphans account for street children. Children living on the street include those being enslaved and trafficked for forced labor and/or sexual exploitation or those forced to serve as child soldiers in wars and conflicts around the globe. There are no written records about these children.

Not all street children are abandoned children. The picture is way more complex than that. Some of these children are not orphans at all. Instead, they are stolen or runaway children whose families are seeking their return. Those children don't count as orphans, but they are intermingled with a significant number of orphans in an indistinguishable mass. Their similarity is that many of them live outside the influence of a family, and they are easily victimized because of a lack of familial ties. In many countries when children go missing, few if any law enforcement resources are leveraged to find them. We have to become involved and lead our churches to become involved in both protecting and caring for these children.

The truth is that estimating the number of street children worldwide is almost impossible. The number that is most often quoted is 100 million worldwide. But this supposed statistic is little more than a guess from a couple of UNICEF reports issued in the 1990s. Later research has led to the reasonable conclusion that there are many fewer street children in the world. Surprisingly, some are still well connected to their families and not in need of the kind of care that we might suppose. Like the rest of the discussion about the number of orphaned and vulnerable children, we don't need to fall prey to hyperbole. There are likely several million—not 100 million—including those who are documented and undocumented orphans.

This notion does not minimize the crisis or simplify the task. It merely focuses us. The presence of one uncared-for street child in the world merits our attentiveness in Jesus' name. Whatever the number is, the Bible is clear that we have an obligation to find ways to care for them all. We have to use the best of all that God has given us to come to solid answers.

The problem of street children is one of the most difficult issues to solve in the orphan crisis because of the lack of documentation of many of these children. On paper, a great many of them do not exist. The ones that do not have families and could be adopted are beyond the reach of traditional adoption care because they lack documentation. Their governments must either figure out ways to document them and to facilitate their adoption through traditional channels, or we must begin to work with the church to find the best care solutions for them, regardless of their documentation.

INSTITUTIONALIZED CHILDREN

As mentioned previously, there are an estimated 10 million orphans living in institutions worldwide. These children are institutionalized for a variety of reasons. Some are there because of the inability of their families to care for them. Those reasons often include everything from family dysfunction to poverty to a disabling condition, either the child's or the parents'. Others are there because they have nowhere else to go, having lost their parents to death or abandonment and being without other relatives who are able to provide them a stable home and support.

The institutions these children are growing up in are as complex and different as the children who inhabit them and the circumstances that brought them there. Around the world, you can find everything from government-run orphanages to private group homes run by nongovernment organizations (NGOs). The philosophies of care these institutions operate under are as varied as the entities that have created and sponsor them.

A self-contained ecosystem. The children eat, sleep, play, receive basic medical treatment, and even go to school all in the confines of the orphanage. All the children know of life is viewed through the lens of the institution until the day they are launched into independence. In these cases, the focus of the institution isn't on preparing them for life after their time there; it is on running an efficient day-to-day operation with as few problems as possible. This means that things like laundry, meal preparation, and so on, are done en masse by a staff of caregivers. The children are given little real freedom and are not taught much responsibility that prepares them for an independent life. Moreover, the need to run an efficient organization on a large scale breeds something that always tends to have a hardened, policy-over-people feel.

In my experience from getting to know postinstitutionalized older orphans, I have learned that they tend to talk about an entire subculture that existed outside of the purview of their caregivers. Some of what they talk about is pretty benign. Nothing more than the kind of cliques and hazing you would expect to find among most American middle schoolers and high schoolers, but some of the rest is quite shocking. What is more shocking is that the stories aren't just from kids who lived in large government-run institutions. These same problems can be present in very well-intentioned and seemingly well-run NGO institutions as well.

The problems occur when children who come to the institution with profound needs and hurts (and even backgrounds of physical, emotional, and sexual abuse) are put into an institution where there is both inadequate care for their underlying hurts and inadequate supervision.

At the end of the day, institutions are necessary. They are a crucial link in the orphan-care chain. At times, they are the only response to the immediacy of a crisis that creates a massive number of new orphans, such as a civil war or a natural disaster. Other times, they may be the best solution to a worse situation. A home for severely physically and/or mentally challenged children is necessary in a country that otherwise lacks the infrastructure to deal with such conditions. Nevertheless, nearly all who have a stake in the worldwide orphan-care conversation agree that institutional care should be a short-term, last-resort option for children whenever possible.

WHERE TO GO FROM HERE

As you can see, the issue of how we are to respond to orphans around the globe is complex. There is no one-size-fits-all solution to the global orphan crisis. Understanding a biblical basis for our action helps to give us a basis for action, but how we should respond is the question.

All of the issues presented here impact how we as the church respond to our responsibility to care for orphans. We must attempt to understand the total picture of these orphans and their context and adapt to the ever-changing world in which we minister. At the same time, we are waging a war that calls for clear and careful action on behalf of the Most High God. I think we are not to see these two outcomes as competing goals or balancing tensions but rather simultaneous objectives that ultimately serve to increase the fame of God as the defender of the defenseless. To begin to reach these objectives, we must strive to understand more fully God's heart for orphans. Once we have come to know God and His motivation more, we can understand our task in the work of orphan care in its most complete sense.

God Is Moving: Orphan Care and Adoption Across the Globe

I DO NOT REALLY KNOW WHAT IT IS LIKE TO BE PART of a revival or another special outpouring of God's Spirit. Over the last few years, I have spent some time with friends who have experienced some extraordinary outpourings of the Holy Spirit in their ministries, and one thing has struck me about their recollections of those movements. They were all aware that they were witnessing God do something out of the ordinary for His glory, but they weren't fully aware of just how special it was or how far-reaching the move of God was until long after the movement itself had passed. I think we are in the midst of one of those moments right now, and it is sweeping across the globe.

Having had the privilege to see a lot of what is happening around the globe for orphans at the meta-level, I am convinced the church is beginning to be swept up in that kind of movement of His Spirit in a revival of concern for the fatherless that will radically change us and our world.

I come from a tradition where talk of movements of the Holy Spirit and the breaking out of revival can make folks a little nervous. Frankly, we are not known for being very free when it comes to the charismatic, so it is really extraordinary to have had a front-row seat to what has been taking place in the last few years. All over the world, in simultaneous little explosions of awakening, God has been waking up the church to the needs of orphans, but also He has been reacquainting the church with that oft-forgotten aspect of His character as defender and protector. Through the church's renewed passion for the fatherless and the vulnerable, He is giving a renewed voice to the gospel to many among the nations of the world. That voice is coming, not from missionaries who care for orphans in their midst or foreigners who adopt, but from national churches that are answering the call to care for orphans among their own people. God is planting a dream in His church that is rooted in the vision that He has given us for His coming kingdom: a world without orphans.

IS IT POSSIBLE?

Will we ever see a world without orphans? The answer is an emphatic yes! And, for even better news, I can tell you *when* we will see it. We will see the world rid of its orphan problem when the Son of man returns and reestablishes His kingdom. That's not just theological doublespeak. It is a reality that should impact our daily thoughts and actions.

The most dominant theme in the Gospels is the kingdom of God. The majority of folks around Jesus misunderstood. Most expected an earthly kingdom to be established while He was on earth the first time. The Jewish leaders of the day were so threatened by this misunderstanding that they turned Him in to the Romans as a revolutionary rebel and had Him executed as a threat to the state.

They didn't understand that Jesus always talked with a different sense of time and space. After all, He wasn't limited by either, except in the brief moment that He had chosen to take on human limitations and dwell with us. In Ephesians, we learn that our adoption as children of God was established "before the foundation of the world" (Ephesians 1:4). Jesus didn't limit His teaching about His kingdom in chronological terms. He described it as having an already-but-not-yet quality. That means that the conditions of living under the rule and reign of Christ are true and fulfilled now, but they will be truer and more fulfilled later.

Jesus intends that, as His disciples, we will ease the temporal suffering of people, giving the world a taste of the coming re-creation and restoration that He will usher in as He establishes His kingdom at His second coming. That is part of the gospel story too, and that is part of what we have to announce about Him as King. When we are working to prevent poverty and disease and fatherless children and when we are telling people how to find peace with God through Christ's sacrifice for the sins of the world, we are extending His mission. We must also realize that those ministries will never be completely successful. Jesus said so. Remember what happened when a woman anointed Jesus with some precious oil?

> *Now when Jesus was at Bethany in the house of Simon the leper, a woman came up to him with an alabaster flask of very expensive ointment, and she poured it on his head as he reclined at table. And when the disciples saw it, they were indignant, saying, "Why this waste? For this could have been sold for a large sum and given to the poor." But Jesus, aware of this, said to them, "Why do you trouble the woman? For she has done a beautiful thing to me. For you always have the poor with you, but you will not always have me. In pouring this ointment on*

my body, she has done it to prepare me for burial.
Truly, I say to you, wherever this gospel is pro-
claimed in the whole world, what she has done will
also be told in memory of her" (Matthew 26:6–13).

Jesus spoke a profound truth about poverty—and suffering, in general—in this passage. As long as we are living in a world broken by sin, we will never eradicate suffering. This is part of the futility that Jesus saves us from. He is coming again, and He will establish a kingdom that will set right what was broken when sin entered the world.

Remember all that talk in chapter 2 about widows, orphans, and sojourners? Well, we have returned to that subject here; only the focus is at the end of the gospel story. God will deal with all three once and for all by ending all suffering. Until then we have a mission to tell people everywhere of His first coming and to represent the life change that He brings. We do this by doing good works to end the suffering that causes children to become orphans and to help children who are orphans.

Without becoming too apocalyptic or pulling out a bunch of charts and graphs, I am convinced that we are closer to the establishing of Jesus' kingdom today than ever before. Why? Scripture and common sense. Jesus said He would come again personally to establish His kingdom. He hasn't yet, but the signs of His kingdom's coming are literally breaking out in the care for orphans and vulnerable children all across the globe.

THE SAME, ONLY DIFFERENT

Just before Jesus ascended to heaven, He gave a pattern for the movement of the gospel across the globe (Acts 1:8). He told His followers that the good news would first spread to Jerusalem, then to Judea and Samaria, and finally to the rest of the world.

In a similar way the gospel spread from Jerusalem in the first century, a gospel-centered movement focused on ending the global orphan crisis is spreading across the globe. Churches, ministries, and individuals are coming together to pursue the goal of a world without orphans for the glory of Christ. One difference in this movement is that it doesn't have one Jerusalem, or starting point, but many. There are many little epicenters of God's movement popping up all across the globe with their effects extending out like the ripples from a pebble cast into a pond. More and more, we are seeing the effects of these seemingly unrelated, disconnected movements intersect like a tapestry being woven by God. Another difference is that there is not a new or more complete message to give to the world. Jesus' disciples had the rest of the story to tell in the gospel. That is different from what we see happening. Orphan-care and adoption ministry has been going on for a long time, and so many have toiled away for Christ in anonymity. What has changed is that God is pouring out His Spirit, but He is doing it in a way that seems strikingly familiar to the way He ushered in the first coming of His Son. Just as God didn't use Rome as the theater for Jesus' story to unfold, He is using some unlikely places to bring revival to His church through caring for orphans.

ORPHAN SUNDAY

God has been working profoundly in the lives of His church in Africa. Believers are overcoming the cultural stigma of orphans and

What we have seen is that desperate people who are overwhelmed by the plight of orphans call out to God and He shows up.

embracing the gospel-centered ministry of orphan care. Christian believers are adopting and caring for fatherless children and integrating them into their churches.

What we know as Orphan Sunday began much earlier than the more organized Christian Alliance for Orphans (CAFO) or World Without Orphans (WWO) and in a place you may not imagine. Orphan Sunday is now perhaps the most recognized aspect of God's working in the worldwide orphan-care movement, but the movement's roots are not in an organized or institutionalized effort. Rather, Orphan Sunday began rather inauspiciously in one little church in Kalingalinga, Zambia, with a mighty move of God's Spirit.

Pastor Billy Chondwe saw the plight of orphans, widows, and other vulnerable people in the area around his church in Zambia. Though he pastored a poor church, he was convinced that the gospel compelled his church to respond actively to the needs of the vulnerable. He led the church to set aside an Orphan Sunday to focus on God's heart for orphans and to take up an offering to help them. The church responded and even met immediate needs in their midst that day. Providentially, God had Gary Schneider of Every Orphan's Hope in that service in Kalingalinga that day to witness what He did through that little church. Gary brought the message and the idea of Orphan Sunday back to America and shared it. Ultimately, he shared it with the Christian Alliance for Orphans and through their platform, Orphan Sunday has become a worldwide day of focus for thousands upon thousands of churches and hundreds of thousands of people. God is waking up His church.

POCKETS OF AWAKENING

To try a give a full description of everything that God is doing around the world to awaken His church to care for orphans is impossible. The pace that the segments of this movement are springing up is too rapid to be chronicled. Often these little movements have the feel of being organic and isolated and not particularly well planned or strategically assembled. Most often the strategies and plans come later—once the movements are well under way. What we have seen is that desperate people who are overwhelmed by the plight of orphans call out to God and He shows up. Something happens to provide for orphans that is out of the norm or stretches the paradigm of convention beyond its limits. A movement begins and many join the work. Essentially, this is what happened in Pastor Billy's church and what has happened in many other places. At times trying to remember the people, the places, and the stories of the various little movements that make up the big sweeping movement can be confusing. But we can be confident that God isn't confused.

To bring some sense of clarity to our understanding of this worldwide movement, I want to tell you a few stories of how God is using a couple of organizations to catalyze the spread of this movement to care for orphans by His church. One of the organizations, known simply as the World Without Orphans movement, is comprised of loosely connected regional and national World Without Orphan alliances from all over the world.

———— ✸ ————

The initial vision for the World Without Orphans movement came from what might be the unlikeliest of places: Ukraine. In transition since the dissolution of the former Soviet Union, the nation (about the size of Texas) is the home to about 30,000 adoptable orphans and 30,000 Christian churches. In 2009, a small group of pastors and Christian leaders began meeting together to pray and to discuss Ukraine's orphan crisis. In one of those meetings, Mykola Kuleba, chief of Kyiv city Child Protection Service, prayed that Ukraine would become "a nation without orphans." God used this simple prayer as the galvanizing vision for the group, and they began working and praying around the possibility of forming an Alliance for Ukraine Without Orphans. Together, these leaders calculated that if just one family in each church in Ukraine adopted an orphan, the orphanages would be emptied. It was their dream to see Ukraine become the first country in the world where national Christians would empty orphanages by adopting all the children. According to Ruslan Maliuta, the president of the Alliance for Ukraine Without Orphans,

From the very beginning, we were focused on the idea that it would be a joint effort, that no one organization would control it. Another thing that was clear was that it was about getting the church mobilized. We all had experience working with the government, with nongovernment (NGO) organizations, but we agreed that this vision would only come into reality when the body of Christ would take responsibility. We agreed that the key component was getting the church engaged and focusing on the spiritual part of caring for orphans.

Officially launched in November 2010, the Alliance for Ukraine Without Orphans has already had a major transformative impact on Ukraine that is rippling out from this little Eastern European nation like waves from a tsunami. Locally, the number of adoptions by Ukrainians is growing every year, and foster care is growing. From 2004 to 2012, the number of children in foster care has grown to 12,000. There is a waiting list for Ukrainian families wanting to adopt children under the age of seven, and most orphaned children are now being placed into families instead of going to orphanages. Subjectively, I have seen dramatic evidence for this as orphanages that I have worked in over the last decade are being consolidated and are closing because the population of children they need to serve has plummeted in the last three to four years. The number of babies who are abandoned in birth hospitals also decreased 50 percent in the last four years. This type of concern and care for orphans is unprecedented in Eastern Europe. Indifference is turning into defense and protection.

―⸻―

THE MOVEMENT SPREADS

Following the Acts 1:8 pattern, the spark from Ukraine has spread to believers in other countries, leading them to start their own "without orphans" movements: Russia Without Orphans, Belarus Without Orphans, Romania Without Orphans, and Latvia Without Orphans. It is amazing to watch how the vision for providing a home for every orphan has caught fire in the hearts of believers in different places of the world. It has been an organic process in which believers and churches have responded to God's movement in Ukraine. Local believers in these places have taken the models begun in Ukraine and adapted appropriately. Each of these national movements is comprised of clusters of local and regional orphan ministries dedicated to a strategy to *inform, mobilize,* and *equip* in order to engage and involve local churches. Maliuta says,

"We believe that this vision has the power to transform nations and it is our hearts' desire that this movement would catch hold around the world, and that believers across the globe would unite to fight for a world without orphans."

The advent of Russia Without Orphans is particularly noteworthy in light of the Russian Federation's decision to halt adoptions to the United States. God was at work in the hearts of His church long before the adoption ban was on the hearts of Russian officials. As Joseph said to his brothers in Genesis 50:20, "As for you, you meant evil against me, but God meant it for good." Accordingly, the Russian church is stepping up to care for orphans and putting the gospel on display within their culture.

Increasingly, Russian political rhetoric has centered on the theme that the ban on American adoptions is in the best interests of Russian orphans because it is intended to serve as a catalyst for Russians to care for orphans. To that end, the Russian government has contrived a system of financial incentives for foster care and adoption *coincidentally* called Russia Without Orphans. According to early reviews, the government system is riddled with corruption and is an abject failure.

In contrast, the faith-based Russia Without Orphans movement is increasingly successful. Families from churches are willing to adopt and foster regardless of financial incentive. Russian churches are observing Orphan Sunday and praying for the needs of orphans and vulnerable children. Russia Without Orphans has begun hosting an annual conference. In March 2013, 157 delegates from 38 regions of the Russian Federation and six countries gathered in Moscow to make recommendations on addressing the orphan crisis in Russia. The resulting *Joint Action Plan of Russia Without Orphans* has even been received by the Russian Federation's Public Chamber, Federation Council, and State Duma for consideration by the government in policymaking. God's movement is rippling out from beyond Eastern Europe to the far reaches of the globe.

Ukraine Without Orphans and the alliances it has spawned are not just a project or an organization. Instead, they represent a vision that Christians around the world can have a significant impact on the orphan challenge. It is an acknowledgment that God is moving through His church around the world, and He desires that every child would grow and flourish in a loving, permanent family and know their heavenly Father.

A WORLD WITHOUT ORPHANS

The leadership of Ukraine Without Orphans joined with leaders of the 4/14 Window Movement to consider how a global movement for orphans could enhance the 4/14 Window's mission of changing the global church's view of children and their rightful place in God's kingdom. As a result, 45 delegates representing 15 countries, people from every continent but South America met to work on developing the World Without Orphans (WWO) global orphan-care initiative as part of the 4/14 Window Movement's Transform World Global Challenges Summit in November 2012. Over the workdays, the leaders refined the vision of WWO and created a seven-year action plan for the World Without Orphans effort to promote the placement of children in families within their local contexts. This plan prioritizes family-based orphan care, including reunification efforts and kinship care to prevent vulnerable children from becoming orphans, as well as adoption and family-like orphan-care solutions.

⟳

GLOBAL MOVEMENTS INITIATIVE

The Christian Alliance for Orphans (CAFO) began the Global Movements Initiative in 2012. Believing that seeing the national church rise within a country is the primary answer to the global orphan crisis, CAFO initiated the Global Movements Initiative specifically to catalyze and support this type of work throughout the world. Under the direction of David Hennessey, CAFO's director for Global Movements, the Global Movements Initiative has begun to connect previously disconnected orphan-care ministries and projects and to consolidate previously unconsolidated movements.

In 2013, CAFO hosted a two-day Global Leadership Forum prior to the annual CAFO Summit 9 in Nashville, Tennessee, that was attended by a broad diversity of leaders from every continent but South America. This forum established a working set of biblical leadership qualities to replicate in leaders. They also began establishing a set of best practices and practical skills to guide the development and leadership of national orphan-care alliances. Finally, the group gathered a smaller working group of key international leaders to take steps toward establishing an autonomous Global Orphan Care Council comprised of orphan-care leaders from around the world. In a short time, the work of the CAFO Global Movements Initiative promises to yield huge kingdom results in helping the church to respond well to James 1:27.

PRESSED DOWN, SHAKEN TOGETHER

The blessings of God in this movement are abundant, and they continue to flow. And, more and more the strands of ministry are beginning to connect. For example, the Eastern Africa Orphans Summit first convened in 2011 in Kenya. They met to pray and consider how to mobilize the local African church to care for orphans in greater numbers. God is creating a burden for adoption within His church to bring orphans into families. What began as primarily a gathering of people doing orphan ministry in Nairobi extended to all of Kenya and beyond. The most recent conference in 2013 brought together African Christians from six countries, including Kenya, Zambia, Uganda, and South Africa. In addition to meeting to pray and learn, the leaders came together to brainstorm how to accomplish the work and to share stories of how God is changing lives for His glory.

One great development came from pastor Billy Chondwe, the pastor through whom God birthed Orphan Sunday. It seems God is using Pastor Billy again. He has relocated from Zambia to South Africa to attend seminary, and God has given him a new vision. God has led Pastor Billy to envision a movement among the 18 countries of the southern African region, so he began contacting leaders and casting a vision for ministering to orphans in each of those nations. There is an emerging plan for a southern African summit in June of 2014 that will likely involve more than 800 African believers from these 18 nations coming together to seek God's face over spreading the gospel and caring for orphans. God is defending orphans for His glory and for the sake of His gospel in a powerful way!

BEYOND EUROPE AND AFRICA

Additionally in the summer of 2013, conferences of pastors and leaders were held in Guatemala, Bangladesh, and India. The theme was constant: praying for God to awaken a heart among His people to care for orphans by adoption and home-based care from within their cultures. These movements are exciting. For when the church rises up within a culture and begins to care for the voiceless and the defenseless, the church not only eases earthly suffering but also paints a living picture of the gospel for its neighbors.

The stories presented in this chapter barely scratch the surface of all that God is doing around the globe through His church to care for orphans for His glory, but I think they are sufficient for you to see that something is building. An unprecedented coming together is happening right before our eyes. Churches and ministries are laying down their individual agendas for the common goals of caring for orphans and demonstrating the gospel. What has not happened for years is happening right before our eyes, and the stories are amazing, inspiring, and instructive. In the next chapter, I will share a few of them with you, to help you consider your place in the global orphan-care movement.

Chapter 6

Stories of God's Movement Among the Nations

ONE OF THE GREAT JOYS OF THE JOURNEY OF progressively understanding all that God is doing among the nations for orphans and vulnerable children has been the extraordinary things that I have witnessed God accomplishing through His people for His glory. These people and their stories are inspirational. They are inherently ordinary people through whom God is accomplishing extraordinary things. I hope as you read some of the details of their ministries that you will find ideas to act upon and encouragement to start something to aid the fatherless using the gifts, resources, and relationships with which God has blessed you.

HOPEHOUSE INTERNATIONAL

Of all the ministries that I have encountered, one of my favorites is HopeHouse International®. The ministry of HopeHouse began in Ukraine before the fall of the former Soviet Union, during perestroika. Originally, their ministry was established with touring groups of Christian musicians, including singers and orchestras who entered the newly open Communist nation to spread the gospel through the musical arts. These touring groups commonly ministered in the many orphanages around the cities where they were performing. Lacking adequate highway transportation and hotel accommodations for a large touring group, these entrepreneurial missionaries employed large boats for housing and transporting the musicians to their engagements and to serve orphans across Ukraine.

Times changed, and ministry needs changed also. As the Soviet Union gave way to a series of independent states, the needs of orphans became a pressing concern. Deneen Turner and Yuri Yakovlyev, cofounders of HopeHouse, refocused the ministry to care for orphans through facilitating adoptions. Sensing God's leadership, they believed helping Ukrainian Christian families adopt should be their focus. To accomplish this goal, HopeHouse works in partnership with local church pastors to identify families who are seeking to adopt. In exchange for a family's commitment to adopt three or more children and a church's commitment to support the family with community and encouragement, HopeHouse agrees to provide the family a house!

Frankly, I have to admit that I was skeptical when I first heard the HopeHouse ministry model. I had heard stories of past abuses of the domestic adoption system in Ukraine, such as families adopting children from an orphanage in one area to get a government bonus only to relinquish them to an orphanage in another area weeks later. So I had my doubts. But, to God be the glory, the HopeHouse model is working! In the 13 years that they have been in existence, HopeHouse has eradicated the equivalent to roughly five Ukrainian orphanages through adoption and have had exactly *no* failed adoptions!

Another way that HopeHouse gives people and churches an opportunity to join in to the work to build homes is by allowing volunteers to help build a house. Construction teams are welcomed to Ukraine to start and finish homes. These teams have some limited opportunity to engage orphans, but the primary purpose of these trips is to build houses for the families who are adopting.

This past February, I attended HopeHouse's Evening of Hope and had an opportunity to hear from one of the young women who is part of the first family adopted into a HopeHouse home. Now, years later, she is a wife and mother and a graduate of the Southern Baptist Theological Seminary in Louisville, Kentucky. Wow! The investment that God has been making among the nations for His glory is immense, and it is growing. As Ruslan Maliuta of World Without Orphans said,

> "It's not as if things like this have not been going on for years. There are many people, both foreigners and nationals, who have been working away for years and really making a difference, but it seems that God is moving in a special way to show us something special about Himself."

Ministries like HopeHouse are showing us both God's profound sovereignty and His strategic nature. God is working, and we just have to catch up to where He already is and join Him there.

LIFESONG FOR ORPHANS

Lifesong for Orphans has national partnerships in Central America, South America, Africa, Asia, and Eastern Europe. Each initiative is as different as the country and the partner it involves, but each fulfills Lifesong's mission to "bring joy and purpose to orphans" and is accomplished by making sure children they serve will have:

- No want for food, clothing, medical care, or shelter
- Fundamental Christian training and discipleship
- Quality education to provide a foundation for the future
- Continued love and support as they transition into adult living

UKRAINE

I have had some personal experience with some of Lifesong's work in Eastern Europe. In Ukraine, one of their initiatives is to create a Constant Christian Presence (CCP) in state-run orphanages. This CCP happens when a church provides the resources for a Christian worker (sometimes even an orphanage employee) to be trained to disciple the children, teach them life skills, foster their connections with local churches, and help prepare them for life beyond the orphanage. There are currently more than 1,000 children being mentored through the Lifesong CCP program by Ukrainian Christians with the support of US Christians. The goals of this program are simple and immediate. They are to encourage local churches to cultivate long-term, continual connections with orphans and orphanages with the hope that these actions will produce an immediate impact on children who are living in and graduating from the system. The program is using resources from other international partners to fund and facilitate this work and make sure that fewer children slip through what is an overwhelmed and highly bureaucratic system.

Lifesong continues to support orphan graduates as they transition to adulthood by providing transition homes. I have had the privilege of being involved in a Lifesong project to build a permanent transition home for orphan graduates in the region of Zaporizhia.

Orphans in Ukraine are released from institutions at ages 16 to 18. Many leave the institutions being a year or two shy of completing secondary school or being qualified to enter a trade school. Although the government provides an apartment and a stipend, the children are often not prepared to handle the responsibility of independent life, and the conditions of the accommodations they are given are deplorable.

By contrast, transition homes provided by ministries create the atmosphere of a spiritual and relational *greenhouse* for graduates. They live in a nurturing family-like environment, learn basic life skills, and become prepared to transition into adulthood. The living conditions are safe and healthy. The children learn vocational skills or continue to pursue an education, and they can continue to grow in Christ through a consistent relationship with their houseparents and families in the partnering churches from the surrounding community. The "Zap" home, as it is affectionately known, is just one of several transition homes that Lifesong operates in the country.

Ukrainian Domestic Adoption

Lifesong is also helping to get orphans out of the system through domestic adoptions. Adoption Without Borders is the name of the program that Lifesong started to create holistic partnership between Ukrainians and American churches and individuals. The program essentially comes alongside couples in Ukraine who are seeking to adopt but who run into red-tape barriers and might need financial assistance in order to complete their adoption.

While it may cost upwards of $35,000 for a US family to adopt an orphan from the Ukraine, churches or individuals can give $500 and fully facilitate a Ukrainian indigenous adoption. That amount is often all that is needed for a Ukrainian family to make basic alterations to their home to meet Ukrainian governmental regulations or to pay for legal assistance with paperwork. As you might expect, Lifesong has seen many people interested in helping with these indigenous adoptions. In Ukraine, Lifesong staff members have helped place more than 140 Ukrainian orphans into Ukrainian Christian families—that's the equivalent of emptying a typical orphanage and placing every child into permanent loving families. Additionally, Lifesong provides excellent connection-based pre- and postadoptive training and support for these families, as well as maintaining solid relationships with the local orphanages, governments, courts, and churches to continue to perpetuate the process long into the future. For a church or family in many parts of the world, $500 can be raised or given very easily, but for a family in Ukraine that generosity can literally be the gift that allows the dream of adoption to become a reality.

ETHIOPIA

In Ziway, Ethiopia, Lifesong tried something new. *Instead of building orphanages*, they thought, *how could we keep families together? Instead of accepting the cycle of poverty, how can we help to break it? Instead of increasing dependence, how can we create a path to self-sufficiency?*

The plan they came up with was simple. Feed these kids twice a day and help families to stay together. Give them an incredible education, equipping them to break the cycle of poverty. Additionally, mentor and grow these kids so they can become the future leaders of Ethiopia.

The plan is working.

In 2009, there were 230 students at the Lifesong schools. Churches, business people, and individuals generously helped build more classrooms in 2011, and the number grew to 570. That momentum continued and Lifesong has built even more classrooms. As this was being written in 2013, school just started with 830 children attending. The school is on its way to three campuses with 1,580 students.

Together with Ethiopian partners, Lifesong for Orphans is building a school system that can generate 140 leaders every year. These future leaders will be equipped to transform their country and their continent from the inside out and drastically alter Africa's orphan and vulnerable child cycle in this region.

ONE HOPE

Christian Vision is a United Kingdom-based charity that was created by Lord Edmiston in 1988. One of the branches of Christian Vision is called Impact a Nation and, according to the charity's website, Impact a Nation's

> Projects work on a national scale by training local leaders and carrying out activities to positively impact and contribute to society. These projects aim to significantly impact the local community and include the following activities: education, health care, skills training, church development, and humanitarian projects.

One of Christian Vision's projects under the Impact a Nation branch is an initiative in Ukraine called One Hope. Under the leadership of Peter Billingham, a former British pastor; Ukrainian nationals, Pavel Gladchenko and Lena Smal, One Hope has gathered an impressive staff of national believers to pursue one goal: to provide a mentor for each orphan in Ukraine. The mentors build a relationship with a specific child by visiting on a regular basis and by special visits on weekends or holidays. Also, the mentoring relationship extends to the child being given the opportunity to spend time living in the family of his or her mentor. Their purpose is simple: to prepare orphans residing in boarding schools and orphanages for independent life through mentoring. The One Hope slogan sums up how their theology leads to philosophy and gives way to action: "Our Children. Our Future. Our Responsibility."

One Hope began in the Ukrainian capital of Kyiv in collaboration with the Kyiv City Service for Children. By having staff workers who are trained professionals in the areas of social work, education, and psychology, One Hope has provided credible ministry in training projects that now extend across Ukraine. Program mentors are prepared to engage in relationships with mentees that teach life skills and spiritual values and help them reach their potential as adults. The long-range goal of One Hope is to provide a mentor for each of Ukraine's estimated 70,000 orphans and vulnerable children living in government-run institutions.

This ministry is a fantastic example of how God can use a spark like Christian Vision to catalyze the resources that exist within a nation for its good and for His glory with the contribution of just a few resources and given an opportunity. What has impressed me most about the ministry model of Christian Vision is their investment in raising up young visionary leaders from within Ukraine to lead the nation and the church into the future. They are gaining traction through *franchising* their model by giving it away to others, and the gospel is going forth as a result. As a result of their open-handed approach to ministry, One Hope has seen ten more projects born or in development using their model. None of these new ministries are under One Hope's authority. One Hope continues relating to and supporting these groups with training and development, but their unselfish kingdom vision has resulted in more than 250 additional mentors. They have almost as many orphan mentees outside their actual ministry purview as within it.

Much like the rest of what God has begun in other areas of orphan care in Ukraine, the ministry of One Hope is expanding beyond Ukrainian borders. A mentoring training project has begun in Belarus. My prayer is that more churches will discover this ministry model to provide pastoral care for kids in institutional environments through Christian mentoring. I also hope that American churches with Eastern European partner church connections will help to close the loop by emphasizing the availability of healthy, established resources such as these.

HELP ONE NOW

In 2007, God changed the course of Chris Marlow's life on the streets of Zimbabwe. While on a trip for community development work, Chris was approached by a starving young boy who asked for help. Chris rebuffed him. Later that day, he found himself watching from inside a church-supported compound where 30 rescued children lived and many more were forced to leave because there was no room for them in the safety of the compound. God used those experiences to challenge Chris at his core. He said of himself at the time, "I had planted churches.

I had some successes and had some failures. I talked the missional talk. I myself grew up fatherless, but I realized I was that guy that had done nothing to solve these bigger issues that the world is facing."

God used this experience to send Chris home a different man. After a discussion with the elders in his church and taking advantage of an opportunity for their church plant to become a campus of the Austin Stone Church, God set in motion what has now become Help One Now. Originally working with double orphans in Zimbabwe, Help One Now has expanded work to Uganda and Haiti.

The mission of Help One Now is to be "a catalytic tribe committed to orphans and vulnerable children by empowering and resourcing high-capacity local leaders in order to transform community and break the cycle of extreme poverty." In getting to know Chris and the folks at Help One Now, I have come to believe that their precise mission statement reflects the heart of the ministry itself. They see life in terms of story. According to Chris, "Storytellers are the new prophets and poets. If you can't tell stories, then you can't move the needle at all. Every community has its unique story."

He extends this idea of *story* to explain the skepticism outsiders often have about the church.

> I didn't grow up in the church, so I suppose I am a little skeptical of it. On one hand, the church is portraying this epic story of Jesus, but the level of engagement is so low for most believers. It's like, "If you just do the basics, you'll be fine: Just show up, tithe, serve, and love your family. Give at Thanksgiving and at Christmas, do something

good for the poor." Instead, there is this whole
other narrative that says the world is broken, and
God has given you good gifts to redeem that are
so brilliant and amazing, [but] it's not because
you're worthy. I feel like there's a fear in the
church that if we unleash this potential, then the
church will lose traction.

Help One Now is seeking to tap into a yearning for a fearless,
authentic faith that so many are dying for, and for that faith to
be lived out in the mission of the church.

That sort of gut level honesty that Chris Marlow exhibits,
combined with a fresh, creative spirit, has led Help One Now to
break the typical NGO and parachurch mold. Born from the spirit
of innovation that spurred the development of such ventures as
Charity Water, Invisible Children, and even Tom's Shoes, Help One
Now has drawn on untapped resources of talent and intellectual
capital within the church to address issues such as global poverty,
public health, vulnerable and orphaned children, and human
trafficking from a kingdom-focused perspective.

"How?" we may ask. Chris responds,

I realized there are such high-capacity people
in the church, and the church is boring them to
death because they have no greater mission. So,
when I talked to my friends that were raising $20
million to start an app online they said, "Dude,
I don't want to go be a parking attendant on Sunday morning," And they almost felt bad about
that. The church has to do Ephesians 4. We have
to empower people to serve.

He also said that we need to explore a different way to do missions.

> I think there is so much pent-up passion in the church that is unrealized because the church doesn't know how to empower people to do good works without doing damage along the way. On a Great Commission level, there is so much traction to be gained in the next five to ten years, with the church investing in people with respect to growing their leadership capabilities and capacity. We have to change the traditional missions model. You have some of the most brilliant people who go all over the world for seven to ten days, and they don't put any of their own intelligence to use because the church has locked them into a trip model. . . . What we are trying to do is get these really brilliant, kingdom-focused folks to invest their lives!

Help One Now opens the door for churches to partner with national churches to solve significant problems such as hunger, disease, poor education, and so on, and give voice to the gospel. Churches are encouraged to explore long-term partnerships with churches in other nations in cooperation with Help One Now, with the hope of empowering the best local leaders in developing nations to innovate solutions for their own

This spirit of double contextualization leads to accountability for all partners in the equation.

problems. The role of outside partners is not to set up projects but rather to be a catalyst to innovation and change. For instance, a Help One Now partner in Haiti was made aware of the problem of over-the-border child trafficking. This conversation took eight months, but once one national pastor became convinced of the problem, he was ready to act. Help One Now was able to present him with eight to ten solid models of action from around the world and recommend some action. From there, he is innovating the solution from within, supported by people and ideas from Help One Now church partners.

To this end, Help One Now has established *collectives* of eight to ten professionals to tackle specific issues head-on. For example, one collective assisting Haiti is focused on the issue of high blood pressure among a people group of 50,000-plus people. It is comprised of physicians, physician assistants, nurses, and other medical professionals who meet four to five hours per month and have traveled to Haiti two to three times per year for the past two years to work on the project, supporting national churches. All of this ministry is paving the way for telling the gospel, improving health, and preventing the creation of orphans.

Help One Now's ministry model continues to evolve, and the organization accepts leadership help from its national partners in a healthy way. For example, in the beginning their work focused solely on orphans who had lost both parents. Then, Chris was asked by one of their pastor partners if Help One Now would sponsor a malnourished little girl as part of their program. He said no, based on their plan only to sponsor double orphans. Disappointed, the pastor commented that she would need to be sponsored soon enough. The rebuke of this national pastor led to a change in ministry. This spirit of double contextualization leads to accountability for all partners in the equation. As a result, Help One Now

> *The (Un)adopted program partners are as different as the nations in which they reside.*

engages in sponsorships of orphaned *and* vulnerable children, caring for children in orphanages as well as helping to facilitate family reunifications.

There are all sorts of ways that churches can support Help One Now, from child sponsorships that allow an individual or family to take responsibility for feeding and educating a vulnerable child to a garage sale for orphans that can fund a legacy project at one of the Help One Now children's village partners. Or your church can become a church partner, identifying with a community and investing deeply in the lives of people with good works and the gospel.

LIFELINE'S (UN)ADOPTED

Lifeline Children's Services has been one of my favorite adoption and foster-care providers for many years. I have always appreciated the chief importance of the gospel that permeates all they do as a ministry. Perhaps more than any other single ministry initiative, I have become enthralled with the development of Lifeline's (Un)adopted initiative to help orphans and vulnerable children who are beyond the reach of transnational adoption.

With all that Lifeline was doing to help children through domestic and transnational adoption, executive director Herbie Newell was challenged in his spirit after hearing Pastor Rick Warren speak at the Christian Alliance for Orphans Summit 3.

His talk caused me to ruminate on three points: (1) adoption is not the solution for all orphans and vulnerable children; (2) this is a global problem and needs the attention of the global church; and (3) if there are 153 million orphans in the world, and we are called to care for them, to do so we have to get creative. And we have to be sustainable.

Later in 2008, Herbie Newell and Dave Wood, Lifeline's international director, traveled to Zaporizhia, Ukraine, where they met Katya. They were asked by orphanage workers to try to find an adoptive home for Katya in the US. They did, but upon further investigation found out that she was 16 years old, rendering her unadoptable by American law. They returned to the orphanage in 2009 as Katya was aging out and leaving. The two men realized they had to do something, and Lifeline's (Un)adopted program was born.

This decision came out of a deep conviction that Lifeline's relationship with a country did not exist only to ensure American evangelical Christians the ability to adopt children there. They were aware of the exodus of evangelical orphan-care ministries from Guatemala after the country closed to transnational adoption in 2007, and they vowed to represent Christ and His gospel by ministering to orphans regardless of their adoptability.

As Herbie put it,

> We needed an orphan tool chest. Maybe adoption is the hammer, able to be used in many situations, but it is not always the neatest and best tool. We realized that these children needed ultimately the gospel, but practically they needed life skills,

job skills, mentoring, training, education, and the opportunity to survive outside of institutions and the streets. (Un)Adopted was born to minister to the unadoptable.

They have amassed quite a tool chest since 2009, with nine different organizational partners across five continents. Lifeline's (Un)adopted work focuses on facilitating opportunities for national churches to take care of the children in their own nation. "When a local church has a heart to care for their own vulnerable children, we simply provide them an opportunity to use their gifts and abilities to serve by connecting them with an orphanage," says Garth Thorpe, (Un)adopted's field coordinator. He continues,

"Many times I facilitate in-country meetings with like-minded nationals who desire to care for the fatherless, and then I simply step back and listen to them. When hearts are heard, connections can be made to then care for the vulnerable children of the community."

The catalytic work of (Un)adopted has fanned the flame for orphan ministry in places where resources or local church support has been lacking. But the (Un)adopted program has also encountered some difficulties as they have tried to help without imposing American culture or expectations upon national churches, which are central to (Un)adopted's strategy. As Garth put it, "Bringing the church together to care for children doesn't come from some model or a PowerPoint presentation. It flows from the character of God."

One of the principles distilled from Henry Blackaby's great book *Experiencing God* is to "watch to see where God is at work and join Him there." Lifeline's (Un)adopted staff is truly living out this principle among the nations by connecting orphan ministries, churches, and resources to create meaningful partnerships. (Un)adopted's coordinator, Amy Floyd, explains it this way:

> We have seen that undue pressure has been put on projects (by others). Our partners feel like they have to create something that's bigger and better since Americans are involved. There is always a huge sigh of relief when we tell our partners that's not our heartbeat. We have to continually remind our partners that we want to strive to "go deep, not wide" and do things with excellence. We would rather see 12 children raised up in an environment where they have been discipled and equipped, instead of having 1,000 kids fed without hearing the gospel and being poured into. If we truly want to see the number of orphans lowered, we have to start small so that the next generations are impacted and changed, and so on to the next generations.

The (Un)adopted program partners are as different as the nations in which they reside. In Liberia, a country with many orphans and vulnerable children as it tries to rebuild after years of civil war, (Un)adopted partners with REAP (Restoration of Educational Advancement Programs). REAP conducts gospel-centered camps for orphans from around Liberia. In these camps, the young people learn what it means to establish a biblical foundation and are taught life skills in masonry, sewing, carpentry, and catering. The heart is that, as they grow in their knowledge and love of Christ and have these life skills, they will be equipped to get a job in Liberia. In 2012, some 200 orphans had the opportunity to attend these camps as they tried to transition into a productive adulthood.

In the Dominican Republic, the work of (Un)adopted is much different. There, (Un)adopted has placed a missionary family as full-time ministry ambassadors to coordinate their work. They have formed a strategic partnership between themselves and *Niños de la Luz* (Children of the Light), a ministry that reaches out to street children and offers them hope through the gospel in a variety of ways, including through a family-like boys ranch and *Iglesia Biblica Cristana,* a local church in Puerto Plata. Lifeline coordinates providing supplemental resources, work teams from America, training, and other support as part of its partnership with the local church and the parachurch ministries in the Dominican Republic.

No matter the indigenous culture, the focus of (Un)adopted is to teach the gospel to orphans and vulnerable children who lack families and need support. The ultimate goal is to disciple them to be more like Jesus and to teach them life skills, job skills, enhance their education, and give them an opportunity to live well as independent individuals outside an institution. Their plan involves connecting these kids to local churches and ministries in their own nations as well as sharing help and resources available to them from the American church. For more information as to how to partner with Lifeline's (Un)adopted, check out their website, unadopted.org.

THE PEARL HOUSE

To me, the story of Ghana and God's work among orphans may be one of the most interesting in the world. Osu Castle, the home to the president of Ghana's government in Accra, has a rather long and sordid history. At one time, the castle was one of the largest holding areas for the African slave trade, and the church within the castle was used as the auction floor for a time. From that history lesson, I think there is a haunting caution and reminder to the church of today. Incremental disregard of worship can result in horrific injustices perpetrated by future generations. We cannot afford to repeat these mistakes today. Thankfully, God is paving a way to live out His just heart in Ghana.

Some 275 years later, Ghana is a much different country and Accra is a much different city, but issues of human trafficking and human slavery of another kind still exist. The church's response must be different from its historic one. Every day, scores of young women arrive in Accra either by choice or as victims of coercion from family members or those intending to enslave them in forced labor and/or the sex trade. Many of these girls are as young as their early teens and have traveled 15 to 20 hours from their home regions due to the promise of a better life. What they find is hardly a dream. They find a life on the streets that is nightmarish. Often they survive by carrying heavy loads for people during the day and selling their bodies to men at night. They sleep on the sidewalk or on the hood of a car. Many nights they face beatings, rapes, hunger, and illness. For the most part, these precious young women, who are created after the image of Holy God, are treated as someone else's worthless property.

The Pearl House is a relatively new ministry in Winneba, a coastal town about 45 miles down the coast from Accra. The location is strategic. The Pearl House partners with a collection of local churches that have a heart to go into Accra and rescue enslaved girls but lack the resources to care for them. The goals of the Pearl House are simple. They are seeking to provide a safe home and a family-like environment for vulnerable girls in Ghana by discipling them, teaching them, and giving them a vocational education, connecting them to a local church, and finding them fair and stable employment.

The Pearl House has begun a pilot project that includes 7 girls and has grown to more than 20. Eventually, they would like to expand to a capacity of 50 girls and to plant other Pearl Houses all over Africa. The verse they base their name upon is Matthew 13:45–46, "The kingdom of heaven is like a merchant in search of fine pearls, who, on finding one pearl of great value, went and sold all that he had and bought it." What a way to put the gospel on display and bring a little healing to the awful temporal results of the curse of sin in a place where its effects have historically been so evident!

From almost its inception the vision of bringing justice to the vulnerable and oppressed girls of Ghana, the Pearl House has caught the imagination of students all across America through the ministries of Hello Freedom and evangelist Ed Newton. Hello Freedom is part of the program strategy of Hello Somebody which exists to provide sustainable projects and restorative care to improve the lives of children in need. Hello Somebody supports these cause partnerships by providing consumer relevant products like watches, apparel, and fragrances. The colorful Hello Somebody watch has become a symbol of "active consuming" to many Christian teens in a way similar to the Tom's Shoes trend in the wider culture. Approximately half of the proceeds of each watch sold through this partnership funds the Pearl House's goal of redeeming young women from a life of abuse and victimization.

To sum up the path of the Pearl House, I love the famous quote from the Ghanaian educator Dr. Kwegyri Aggrey: "If you educate a man, you educate an individual. If you educate a woman, you educate a nation."

The Pearl House is giving protection, hope, and education to the victimized, trafficked young women of Ghana, and God is using them to change a nation one life at a time.

There is a common denominator among all the people and ministries whose stories are included in this chapter. None of them set out to build large, successful ministries that someone would write about. In fact, most of them would probably laugh at the impression that they are either very large or very successful. More likely, they would tell you that they are doing the best they can with what they have and feel very blessed. I am confident they would say their successes are a result of God's blessing and their availability not their talent or their skill.

These stories are just a sampling of the stories that could be told of the hundreds of ministries that are doing wonderful work to care for the fatherless. Even with all the ministries that are engaged in caring for orphans, there is so much more to do. I pray that you will draw inspiration from these folks and use it to the fullest to fulfill James 1:27. Whether you join with them or strike out on your own to meet some as yet unmet need, be assured that God has given you something that He can use to serve the fatherless for His glory.

Chapter 7

Growing Up and Gathering Criticism

EVERY MOVEMENT WILL ATTRACT CRITICISM AS IT matures. The evangelical orphan-care and adoption movement is no different. Some of that criticism will be helpful, and some will not be. Some of the criticism of is entirely fair. We have made mistakes along the way. At times, people have rushed out to do seemingly good things in Jesus' name, and yet those good intentions have had bad outcomes. Others have done downright evil things, while calling themselves followers of Jesus, and we repudiate them. Still, some folks find fault with the movement because Christians are seeking ends that are very different than the life goals they seek. In the end, their disapproval is a result of clashing worldviews. We do what we do because of the gospel and a citizenship in the kingdom of heaven. We should not expect that anyone living outside the transformation of the gospel would necessarily agree with or understand our motives. Frankly, we should expect them to be hostile to our agenda at times. As one respected colleague said to me recently, "These are the same people who would be writing books about us if we were doing nothing."

Furthermore, some critics share our worldview but disagree with some of our goals, objectives, or methods. With these individuals, we share a great commonality and discussions are pretty easy. We may disagree over certain nuances of orphan care, but our dialogue with them will likely lead to better answers that will help more orphaned and vulnerable children.

No wanted child should ever be removed from a family because of poverty or some other correctable condition.

No matter the source of the critiques, we must address them. In this chapter, I will focus on several of the more common criticisms of the evangelical orphan-care and adoption movement and give an answer to the critics.

Critique #1: The Crisis Is Inflated by Adoption Demand of Evangelical Christians

One recent criticism of the evangelical orphan-care and adoption movement is that American Christians seeking to adopt are artificially inflating the orphan crisis by increasing the demand for adoptable children in developing nations. The narrative these critics propose is as follows: A nation opens to adoption. Rich foreigners (most of whom are American Christians) come to adopt. Adoption creates economic activity within the developing nation as orphanages, attorneys, hotels, and many others begin to benefit from involvement in adoptions. These developing countries lack infrastructure to handle the influx of adoption activity. When the economic activity from adoption begins, corruption and other unethical practices inevitably follow, as unscrupulous people seeking to profit from the suffering of others swoop in to take advantage of the weak and the poor. Eventually, the atmosphere of adoption causes a backlash as the country tightens adoption laws.

There can be no doubt that to developing nations, adoption by foreigners presents challenges. The opportunities for graft and the pressures on the nation's social services and legal system are substantial. But to lay blame for children being orphaned at the feet of adoptive families or adoption agencies who operate legally and ethically is reckless and irresponsible.

I see two false premises that underlie the assumptions that transnational adoption creates more orphans: First, critics assume that most of these children would be fine without evangelical adoption and orphan-care efforts. With all due respect, how can they be so sure? On one hand, the number of transnational adoptions is easy to track. On the other hand (as I have shown earlier), information that provides an accurate picture of orphaned and vulnerable children is often illusive. Second, critics unfairly fault adoptive parents. Let me put it like this. I am trained as an empirical researcher. In research terms, we would say that adoptive parents can't be demonstrated to be the independent variable, the cause of the effect. The majority of Christians who adopt are not imperialistic bullies set on imposing their will and desires without regard for others. They may unwittingly contribute to a system that is broken, but those who exploit children within a broken system will find other ways that do not involve adoption if adoption is not an available opportunity. To the contrary, most if not all adoptive parents in these situations are law-abiding, ethical people who are seeking the good of the children they are trying to bring into their families.

Transnational adoption critics cite the growing numbers of adoptions in certain nations as evidence of a problem—as if a boom in transnational adoptions is the only problem facing these children. I agree that no wanted child should ever be removed from a family because of poverty or some other correctable condition. But, aside from those conditions, scores of legally adoptable children are awaiting adoption; and where no viable adoption or foster-care options exist in their native countries, there is no arguable reason they should not be transnationally adoptable.

Critique #2: Rampant Corruption in Transnational Adoption

We can't deny that abuses and corruption take place. We shouldn't be surprised by that. The Bible warns us in places like Titus 1:15–16 and Acts 20:28–30 that evil like this will happen in the church and in the world. Remember all that talk about "wolves" appearing as friendly voices. Impostors posing as agents of good and light are nothing new. To be sure, everyone who gets caught up in a corrupt situation isn't a wolf. Some are just well-intentioned people who have been swept up in the mess. But if there is corruption, you can be sure there is a wolf somewhere.

This kind of behavior is common in virtually every type of human suffering and calamity. Earlier this year I had a personal experience that illustrates what I mean, although it had nothing to do with orphans at all. A house we owned in a town where I formerly pastored a church was severely damaged by a tornado. Thankfully, no one was in the house at the time. The next day, I arrived to inspect the damage, and what I found shocked me. I drove through devastation that I cannot describe. Empty spaces strewn with garbage in places where friends' houses used to stand. As I drove closer to my own home, I was an emotional wreck just thinking about people we love and how much they were hurting. Thankfully they were all safe, but many were homeless.

When I reached my house, what I saw took my breath away. Eleven trees were toppled onto our house, and another 12 were down in the yard. These weren't small trees. Nearly all were 100-foot-tall Mississippi pine trees, and the ones on the house had crushed the roof. Torrential rains from the storm were still coming down as I climbed over and under the trees in my backyard.

It was eerily silent in the neighborhood, as police checkpoints kept most people at bay, but suddenly I noticed the sound of crackling pine needles behind me. I turned around to see a smiling but unfamiliar face. The man handed me a business card. He owned a tree service from out of state, and he was offering help. He told me he had the equipment ready and could get the trees off my house by the end of the day. Then he quoted me a price. I thanked him, took his card, and immediately called my insurance adjuster. The adjuster sent a local company to survey the damage that afternoon, and they quoted a price just over *half* the amount of what the "nice" man from out of town had quoted. I think you see where I am going with this. Seeking to profit from disaster and human suffering isn't limited to orphans and adoption. This type of behavior is the self-centered, self-serving action that our fallen nature breeds and that the gospel is intended to repair.

My point in telling this story is that some critics who are lobbing allegations at the evangelical adoption and orphan-care movement are unfairly placing blame at the feet of the wrong people. Corrupt profiteers will always figure out ways to get ill-gotten gain. We cannot deny that corruption has existed and does exist in transnational adoptions. We must stand resolutely and refuse to support that corruption as we adopt and care for orphans. The end does not justify the means.

> *God has given the church the resources to come up with better answers.*

119

In His Sermon on the Mount, Jesus told us that part of being citizens of the kingdom of heaven means living like it right here, right now. We should hold to standards that reflect the holiness of God in all our dealings, and we should insist on ethics from those who represent us in adoptions and work on our behalf in global orphan care.

Remember my earlier reference to the Christian Alliance for Orphans (CAFO)? CAFO is a voluntary association of churches, ministries, and individuals dedicated to "inspire, equip, and reflect God's heart in caring for the orphan in adoption, foster care, and global orphan care initiatives." As part of its membership process CAFO has established standards for doctrine, oversight, and financial accountability. It seems that CAFO has created a good starting point for keeping organizations responsible through its membership process. While some transnational adoption agencies and providers have been implicated in corruption and child trafficking, no CAFO member organizations have ever been implicated.

To that end, I have a couple of ideas that I think would strengthen the transnational adoption process and result in less susceptibility to corruption. I think God has given the church the resources to come up with better answers. History would validate that conclusion. Decades ago when evangelical parachurch ministries were rocked by a number of financial scandals, a group of concerned people and ministries came together to establish standards and to police themselves in such a way as to allow financial contributors to have confidence in ministries again. The Evangelical Council for Financial Accountability (ECFA) was born out of this effort. This was a huge step forward in restoring trust, but moreover it was an example of bright Christian thinkers applying principles of biblical stewardship well to the glory of God and for the good of the church. Today many people won't give to a parachurch ministry unless it is an ECFA member. I think that we have the opportunity to do that same sort of thing with regard to global orphan-care and adoption ministry with a couple of changes to the transnational.

One productive change that has already been made is the passage and implementation of the Universal Accreditation Act of 2012. Beginning in July 2014, adoption agencies that provide transnational adoption services from the United States will have to be accredited according to the standards previously applied only to those agencies accredited to operate in Hague countries. In theory, this law ends the inequity among Hague and non-Hague accredited agencies by applying the same burden of compliance to all agencies as a means of assuring the protection of children and families. The hope is that by having a set of universal standards, ongoing oversight and accountability by agencies will get even better, and the rare cases of graft and abuse of the system will be further eliminated. (We will take a much closer look at the Hague Adoption Convention Standards and Process in chaps. 8 and 9).

After talking with Jedd Medefind, I am thankful to learn of CAFO's creation of a Transparency Project to explore ways to bring greater candidness to the adoption process. The beginning of this project is a document called "12 Questions for Prospective Adoptive Parents to Ask of Adoption Agencies," available at christianalliancefororphans.org. I would like to see CAFO consider going further by asking member agencies to disclose more information about their organizations voluntarily. With this information, adoptive families could evaluate each agency in areas such as policies and practices related to countries served, legal process, ethics, communication, pre- and postadoptive as well as in-country support, current program statistics, theology and doctrine, and a list of references in a single location. Since these agencies provide much of this information to CAFO to qualify for membership, I would suggest they are the logical, impartial entity to curate this information.

I would also recommend that CAFO establish some sort of "gold standard" for transnational adoption agencies that goes beyond the minimum Hague standards. Agencies might receive this special accreditation if they better equip parents to deal with post-placement issues, adhere to stricter ethical guidelines, provide more transparency regarding in-country fees, and so on. I envision a system that polices itself by providing this information about its adoption programs to CAFO and to potential adoptive families who desire to adopt through a CAFO gold-standard agency. With a greater level of scrutiny, the agency would in theory receive more clients because adoptive families would be more assured they are dealing with an ethical agency. Everyone wins.

Many Christians have grown weary of the electoral process, but policymaking can be another area in which Christians can wield positive influence. A perfect example is the way human-trafficking activists and ministries have effectively lobbied the Congress of the United States and the President of the United States to tie US foreign aid funding to a nation's protection of trafficking victims. Why can't we push our government to do the same thing regarding the protection of all families, including adoptive families? The answer is that we can, and we should. In May 2013, Jedd Medefind and others testified before the United States Senate regarding US foreign assistance for children in adversity. Here is a portion of his testimony to the senators about how the US government must engage:

First: priority. We must clearly prioritize family as the ultimate goal for children that currently lack it. By naming "Family Care" as one of its three foundational objectives, the US Action Plan on Children in Adversity helps point our global investments decisively in this direction.

Second: *preservation.* The very best way to guarantee a family for a vulnerable child is to ensure she doesn't lose her family in the first place. On one level, virtually all effective foreign aid—from community development to health projects and microfinance—do contribute to family preservation. But efforts targeting the most vulnerable families on the verge of disintegration are still vital.

Third, *placement.* When preservation or reunification isn't an option, a child deserves a permanent family as soon as is feasible—locally if possible, and via international adoption if not.

All of these are made possible by a **fourth P:** *partnerships* that enable government to cultivate solutions that it cannot create on its own.

To these three principles, we can add three important caveats:

First, although healthy families provide affection and nurture that *systems* can never match, families can sometimes be the source of neglect,

abuse, or worse. Effective child protection systems are always necessary as a check against abusive homes.

Second, commitment to family-based care should
always be complementary—not competitive—to
an equally firm commitment to child protection
and survival efforts. We need not become parti-
sans of either families or broad-based antipoverty
efforts. We can and should champion both.

And *finally,* even as we affirm permanent family
as the ideal, we need not become ideologically
rigid. Anyone who dares to engage the world at
its most broken will sometimes be forced to make
peace with imperfect solutions. We can simul-
taneously work toward the ideal of family . . .
while also affirming the value of residential care
in cases where family care is not currently a feasible option.

In all of this, we can continually affirm and seek to build a broad
continuum of response to the needs of highly vulnerable children.

This continuum always starts with efforts to preserve families
threatened with disintegration and to reunify families that have
been needlessly severed. When it's clearly not possible for a child
to remain safely with his first family, a loving second family is
promptly sought—with relatives or caring neighbors in-country if
possible and via international adoption when local options for
permanent family aren't available. When finding a permanent
new family is not an option, other home-based options become

the priority, including foster care. Finally, when no home-based options are feasible, well-run residential care facilities provide an important alternative far preferable to an abusive home or life on the streets.

I think Jedd is really on to something.

Critique #3: Transracial Adoption to Combat Racist History

Many individuals outside the evangelical community have disparaged transracial adoptions as some sort of misguided plan for dealing with racism and racial reconciliation. Because of what I wrote previously in *Orphanology*, I have been swept up in the controversy as one of the mouthpieces of evangelicalism on this issue. I must say that I feel wholly unqualified, but nonetheless find myself in the middle of the fray.

While I am a father who has adopted children transculturally, I have not adopted transracially. My point in linking transracial adoption and the larger issue of racial reconciliation was not to suggest that transracial adoption is a solution to racial tension or historical racism. On the contrary, I do not advocate adopting transracially out of some ill-conceived racial reconciliation plot. We should adopt because we love children and because Christ loves us. We should adopt for the same reason we should have biological children. We should adopt transracially because God is colorblind and matters of race and culture are outlying concerns according to the Scriptures. We are not trying to prove a point by either adoption in general, or transracial adoption. I think those who are critical have missed the point, and we will never agree because our disagreement is based upon a fundamental difference of worldview.

I am a southern Christian who is aware of our heritage, including the scourge of slavery. I hate how we got here. I hope over the last several years we have demonstrated a repentant heart as a people, but that repentance can never erase our history. Neither can it fully deal with the pockets of sinful racism that still exist, even in some of our churches. We can't run away from our past; we can only try to live differently in our present and shape a different future for ourselves and our children. To God's glory, things are better, especially in the church.

I am proud to serve in a local church where our senior pastor declared recently that the sin of racial prejudice has no place in the church of the Lord Jesus Christ and does not reflect a heart that has been changed by the grace of God through the work of Jesus. I think the heart of our church represents that of most evangelical churches. Many are much farther along in dealing with racial reconciliation in practical matters than others, but I think we are owning our issues and facing them with God's power honestly to His glory.

I grew to adulthood in one of the most racially difficult and divided cities: Memphis, Tennessee, the very site where Martin Luther King Jr. was gunned down in the struggle for civil rights for all people. And although I grew up in a racially diverse environment, race was always recognized as a point of substantial difference, if not division. This bothered me as a young person, and it bothered me more as I became an adult. It didn't seem that race or ethnicity was the most important distinction to God. In his letter to the church at Colossae, Paul says, "Here there is not Greek and Jew, circumcised and uncircumcised, barbarian, Scythian, slave, free; but Christ is all, and in all" (Colossians 3:11). It bothered me because Paul told the church that racial and ethnic differences are tertiary to matters of unity in the gospel. Is he saying that matters of race or culture aren't real or significant? Goodness no! What he is saying is that racial and ethnic differences pale in comparison to the unity and reconciliation that we have in light of the reconciliation we have in Jesus. Should we acknowledge and respect differences of race and ethnicity? Yes, to some degree. Should those differences be of first importance in life? No, we enjoy a bond of brotherhood and sisterhood in Christ that is much closer and more significant.

Should I be surprised that critics outside the church don't understand how we see the distinctions—that they criticize transracial and transnational adoptive families for breaking ethnic and racial barriers to create families? No. Why should we expect that they would interpret the world with a biblical worldview? So, we have to chart a course that acknowledges that racial and cultural differences have some place in orphan and adoption ministry, but they are not nearly the first consideration for us. We also must remember that we will have critics who will not share our convictions because they do not share our Lord, His gospel, or its transformative power. To them we offer patience, but we do not waiver in our commitment to Christ or to care for orphans as the Bible mandates.

As a college freshman, in my college speech class, we studied King's famous "I Have a Dream" speech in great detail. For a kid who had an interest in preaching, I was enthralled with King's preaching and his message. One part of his message rang so true to me that I can remember exactly where I was sitting the first time I heard it. He said:

> I have a dream today.
>
> I have a dream that one day the state of Alabama, whose governor's lips are presently

> dripping with the words of interposition and
> nullification, will be transformed into a situation
> where little black boys and black girls will be able
> to join hands with little white boys and white girls
> and walk together as sisters and brothers. . . .

Praise God, I pray that we are closer to the day King's dream comes true, and I believe that to reach it will require the true metamorphosis that can only come through the real transformation of the gospel. Religion will not do it. Social policy will not do it. Only Jesus can, and I believe He will. I believe I am seeing it happen right in front of me. A conversation with one of my sons reveals the subtle evidence of the seismic shift that is taking place in this generation. I said, "Tell me, bud, which one of your classmates is John?" He proceeded to describe John to me in great detail. I still couldn't imagine his face. Erick went on. *Still nothing.* Eventually he grew impatient with me. Finally, as almost an afterthought, Erick mentioned that John is African American. *How cool,* I thought! It wasn't the first thing my son thought of about John. It was practically the last. It isn't the first thing God thinks of either.

It is more important for a child to have a family than for us to preserve our adopted child's racial and cultural identity, but that doesn't mean we should disregard it. Transracially and transculturally adoptive families are living with one foot planted in each of two worlds. Families cannot separate themselves from their child's story, pretending their children's heritage doesn't exist. In some ways, our kids are truly American, but our kids will always be connected to their country of origin. In our family little bits of Ukrainian culture have permeated our household, and it's no different for any other transnational adoptive family, regardless of racial differences in the family.

As a specialist in adolescent development, I know that one of the most difficult questions that every person deals with: *Who am I?* For adopted kids, the question is a little more complex. Families should consider learning some things about their child's native language, diet, holidays and festivals, and history. By helping them stay connected to their unique heritage, even if we don't know the exact circumstances of their personal story, we can give them a great gift as they are working out the story of their identity. Every family is going to have to discover what will work best personally, but we can celebrate the fact that God has put us together as a family. Our families make delightful pictures of an even truer reality: the unity that God has created in His family through our adoption in Christ.

Another aspect of the critique of transracial adoption is the evangelical adoption community's occasional condemnation of the larger worldwide child welfare community (particularly UNICEF). The criticism has been that they have an agenda to block transnational and transracial adoptions over a misguided preoccupation with ethnicity. Evangelicals agree that we should strive to preserve ethnic and cultural ties, but the best interests of a child are served by getting them into stable, loving homes. Undue delays to try to preserve racial and ethnic ties seem cruel and ethnocentric, particularly when there is little or no hope of family reunification, domestic adoption, or domestic foster care. The long-term negative effects of institutionalization are dramatic, and every month a child spends in even the best institutional care poses a significant risk for developmental delays and poor outcomes later in life.

The international community can come together to deal with this issue. Rather than spend energies hindering transnational adoptions of children who will not be adopted or cared for in their countries of origin, the worldwide child welfare community could dedicate resources to clarify, standardize, streamline, and reduce the cost of adoption in more countries by creating a uniform international process. I believe that would ultimately inhibit a great deal of the corruption. I know there are risks in this strategy and that the likelihood of international consensus is poor, especially in light of the mixed reception of the modest provisions of the Hague Adoption Convention. But it may be a topic for future discussion.

Critique #4: The Overdiagnosis of Foreign Adoptees with Attachment Issues

As a parent of a child who struggles with issues related to attachment, I take these comments very seriously. Having completed much of my graduate education in developmental psychology, I am fairly well versed in the concept of attachment theory. I know that there are a litany of human developmental theorists whose observations all led them to a similar conclusion: children need a stable foundation of love and consistent care from the same reliable caregiver to help them see the world as a good place and to give them a stable foundation to develop everything else—physically, intellectually, emotionally, and socially—for the rest of their lives. That is where some of the agreement falls apart in the psychological world. The question about how much you can go back and make up for what was missed in early life has been a topic of hot debate.

How much can we go back and make up for the damage that has been done in the past? The answer is an emphatic, "We don't know!" What we do know is that we serve a God who is in the business of redemption, taking old things and making them completely new creations. That does not mean that He puts new tread on old tires. It means that He makes new things out of old things or creates from nothing at all. If He can do that in other situations, He can do that with children who have started their lives in tough places. We can't pretend these children aren't different or that they don't have challenges. We can't pretend that their current living conditions are adequate to produce healing or that these circumstances hold the promise of getting better quickly. And we can't stand idly by. So, we have to cling to the hope that God will come to our aid to help us and help them. To families who would adopt older, institutionalized orphans, I would say, "There will be a cost." The longer a child has been in the institution, the greater the cost. The earlier their institutionalization began, the deeper the scars will be. It is almost a given. It does not mean that you should not adopt an older child; it means you should count the cost.

A chorus of credible voices in evangelical adoption circles talk about parenting children who come from hard places—people such as Dr. Karyn Purvis and Dr. David Cross, authors of *The Connected Child: Bringing Hope and Healing to Your Adoptive Family* and developers of the Trust-Based Relational Intervention model with Elizabeth Styffe and Michael Monroe. They teach about understanding the trauma that may have brought these children to this place and how trauma causes the human brain to be wired differently and to respond differently than expected. These specialists have prepared resources that help parents understand how to adjust a child's diet and daily schedule to help them lower stress hormones, how to use a healing voice to talk to a child, and how to trust-build with a child as you parent him or her.

Lots of transnational adoptive parents come home with their child and real life begins to slowly sink in delight. As the high of the first few weeks fades away, the child's special needs start to bubble to the surface as everyone becomes more comfortable with each other. These adjustment problems can be natural, but they can also be unnerving. Knowing what to expect and where to turn in the event of a crisis is crucial. For postinstitutionalized children, one of the needs that often surfaces is some sort of unmet attachment issue that the family may not be expecting because they have not been prepared in advance. This is why preadoption training like that mandated by provisions of the Hague Adoption Convention are so important and why we should think seriously about doing more in this area. Often, the problem can be identifying whether there is a significant problem. A professional therapist may be needed to help navigate that issue, but there are actually very few therapists who are prepared to do that in most communities (especially if there are language and cultural barriers as well).

Sadly, I have seen a scenario like this play out more than once. A family brings a child home, and for the first few weeks, everything is fine. Then, some signs of aggression or other disturbing behavior begin. An already stressed family becomes more stressed. They reach out to local doctors and counselors without much success. In lieu of being able to find competent professional help, where do they go for help? They turn to the quickest source they can access—the Internet! This begins a swapping of stories from one blog to another of one family's experience to another and pretty soon we have the World Wide Web version of the old youth group game "Telegraph" where every adoptive family knows of someone who knows of someone who has a child with RAD (reactive attachment disorder). RAD is a *very* real disorder with long-term consequences for the sufferer and the family of the sufferer, but RAD is complex. I am bothered by much of the alarmist tone of what I have read about RAD on many blogs. I am equally bothered by the critique of RAD as being overdiagnosed like "the attention deficit hyperactivity disorder of the 1990s." The truth is probably somewhere in the middle. Children coming from institutions may have attachment-related issues without having the most extreme expression: reactive attachment disorder.

What we know is that very young children who don't establish a bond with a primary caregiver early in life have trouble establishing a basic sense of trust as a foundation for life. This means that nearly every choice and decision in their lives, both consciously and unconsciously, is made out of a basic sense of mistrust. Fundamentally, they struggle to trust anyone else because they never learned that anyone could be relied upon to change their diapers when they were dirty or wet, to feed them when they were hungry, or to comfort them when they were in distress.

This means that when a child who had a difficult start early in life experiences physical, social, or emotional symptoms related to that difficult start, there are no easy answers. There is no quick-fix behavioral intervention. Nothing you do will instantly unwind all the ways a child may be different. Childhood trauma, neglect, poor nutrition, and even prenatal stress can influence development significantly. For many transnational adoptive families, understanding your child may be a journey that feels a lot like peeling an onion. Going through layer after layer of behavior and painful experience and understanding, you will continue to discover the child whom God has given you.

RESPONDING TO CRITICS

So, how are we to respond? We understand that we have to work with all our hearts in our orphan-care efforts because we are working for the Lord (Colossians 3:23). Orphan care deserves our best because God deserves our best. In humility, we must be ready to listen to the critics and to learn from being challenged. Whether we discover that we are in error or not, the self-reflection and analysis that criticism spurs is ultimately good when it leads us to improve ministry.

Chapter 8

Describing the Indescribable: The Transnational Adoption Process

IF THE TASK OF DESCRIBING TRANSNATIONAL adoption isn't impossible, it is so frustrating that no sane person would ever attempt it. So, in this chapter I will attempt to explain the transnational adoption process and thereby confirm the mental instability that those close to me have suspected for lo these many years!

In all seriousness, accounting for all the variables is the difficulty in trying even to outline the broad contours of the transnational adoption process. Each nation you could potentially adopt from is a distinct, sovereign entity with a unique set of laws and process for adoptions by foreign nationals. To complicate matters, there are variations within the laws of the United States as well. The governments of the Hague Convention on the Protection of Children and Co-operation in Respect of Inter-Country Adoption (Hague Adoption Convention) countries process and oversee adoptions differently than non-Hague Convention countries. The forms and procedures differ from country to country. Adding more complexity, each state in the US has unique laws for adoption that govern everything from home study requirements to postplacement visits and reporting. All this means that it is impossible to answer all the questions (or even anticipate all the questions) that a potential adoptive family may have about transnational adoption.

My objective here is to give you a place to start, from someone who has been there several times personally and has walked through the process alongside numerous families. We have learned a few things along the way that I believe are helpful. Hopefully, you can learn from some of our mistakes and successes, and God will use what is contained in the next several pages to help confirm in your heart whether adopting a child from another country is a way that He desires to grow your family.

WHERE TO BEGIN

My wife, Denise, and I have adopted transnationally three times from Ukraine. In 2003, we adopted our first son at 18 months old. Six years later, we added our second son who was 7 years old. Two years later, our soon-to-be 15-year-old daughter came home. Jokingly, we tell people all the time that we are not the poster parents for transnational adoption. We are more like the crash test dummies!

We love our children deeply, and we know that God has called us to do this, but it is hard. By all conventional wisdom, God built our family all wrong. The birth order is wrong, which has resulted in some special difficulties. We have language barrier problems. We have cultural differences to work through all the time with our two oldest. There are days that it is all a little overwhelming. OK, there are even a few days it is very overwhelming and not even a Calgon bath will take us far enough away. So we just have to pray and keep digging. Fortunately, those days are few and far between.

Nearly everyone I know who is engaged in orphan care and adoption acknowledges the difficulties involved in transnational adoption because most of the children in the world in need of these adoptions are older children and/or children with special needs. Adopting these children is a life-altering commitment for a family. The journey with them can be one of great sacrifice and heartache, as well as fulfillment and joy, guaranteed.

A friend of mine put it well in a recent conversation. I was talking with Ruslan Maliuta, the president of World Without Orphans, who said,

> It's funny, now when I meet people, they ask me not "if" I have adopted but how many I have adopted. People are shocked to know that we have not adopted ourselves. I tell them that adoption is a huge part of orphan care, but it is not the only part. People ask me, "How can you ask people to adopt when you haven't adopted yourself?" I tell them, I don't really ask people to adopt. I share God's heart for orphans and tell them what they can do for orphans. Now that I know everything that I do about adoption, I would not dare ask anyone to adopt. It's like asking someone, "Would you like to be crucified?" It's a similar question. We just don't ask that question. You know that the resurrection is coming, but sometimes in the moment, it doesn't feel that way.

I could not say it better myself. Jesus is the one who asks all believers to take up our crosses daily and follow Him. As pastors or fellow Christians, we don't make that call to people or to each

Continue to pray, become informed, and wait for God to guide you in your next steps.

other, we just echo it. Jesus is the one doing the calling. I think the call to adopt is similar. We should never call anyone else out to adopt. As believers, we all have a responsibility to take the gospel to all nations and to care for orphans as we go as part of that gospel announcement. Adopting is only one way that a few people care for orphans. That doesn't make these people more holy, more special, or more anything. It is just God's plan for their lives.

I have said at many conferences over the last several years that I have a fear for the evangelical orphan-care movement (and for adoptive families, in particular). I fear that adoption will be the evangelical "camp crush" of the moment. You remember those middle school youth camp crushes, right? You went to camp and met a boy/girl and fell madly in love by the second day of camp. On the last day of camp, your world was falling apart, and you didn't see how you could go on as you boarded the bus home. A few weeks later, you could barely remember his or her name. We evangelicals have a terrible history of jumping from one hot cause of the moment to another. We cannot afford to let the orphans of the world down. They have been disappointed enough and, in the name of Jesus, they deserve much more from us. We cannot afford families jumping onto the adoption bandwagon either. I have heard my friend Russ Moore say more than once that we cannot let Christian families rush to adopt like adding another "colorful cause-oriented bracelet to their wrists."

The first thing that I would call you to do as a family considering transnational adoption is to enter into an intense season of prayer. Ask, "What is God leading us to do?" When Denise and I felt a leading to adopt our daughter, we didn't tell anyone. In fact, we were really skeptical. We had just come home with our second son. We were beginning to understand him and his needs, and we knew it was going to be intense. We thought, *God couldn't be calling us to adopt another so soon*. Besides, we were broke. We had just spent everything we had on his adoption. Still, there was something that wouldn't go away. God just continued to nudge, so we prayed quietly. For months we prayed. Actually, there were a lot of times I prayed that God would just take the desire to adopt Nastia away or bring her another family. It would have been easier, but God continued to keep her before us, always in our thoughts.

After about ten months, one of the guys in my small group called me up and asked me out to lunch. We had a kind of accountability relationship. When you are in a relationship like that with a guy, and he calls you up for lunch and tells you he has to talk to you, it can be disconcerting. He wouldn't tell me what he wanted. He just said he had something he wanted to talk to me about. So I went to meet him for lunch at a local Mexican place, and he was sitting in a secluded booth waiting for me. My head was spinning. *What had I done? Was he going to confront me over some sin I was oblivious to or so hardened to that I was unaware of committing?* I was almost sick. There was little small talk. He cut to the chase. He told me that he and his wife had been praying for Denise and me. He said that he had been watching me during some fund-raising that we were doing for an orphan-hosting program where we first met Nastia, and that he kept seeing something in my eyes when I saw her picture. He said he dismissed it at first until his wife mentioned it. Then he just blurted it out, "Is the Lord telling you that you need to adopt Nastia and the only reason you aren't is because of money?"

I broke down and cried like a baby. I unloaded everything that day with him. I found out that his wife was on the phone with Denise having the same conversation at the same time. They walked with us, prayed with us, resourced us, and are like family to us to this day. We saw God provide for us in an amazing way financially, and I know adopting her was the right thing to do. But sometimes it is still hard, having brought a young woman into a family with two young boys. The only thing that keeps me from falling apart some days is the confidence in God's plan and His providence that we were assured of in those early days.

Many families never really struggle with the decision of where to adopt once they have felt the call to adopt; they just come to the process with a sense of calling or an inherent connection. It might be a little like the story of my *Orphanology* coauthor Tony Merida and his wife, Kimberly. Their first adoption was from Ukraine. Their time with our son Erick and Tony's teaching at Kyiv Theological Seminary was a connection that God used for them.

On the other hand, other families enter the process quite open to consider anywhere in the world. So how do you decide? After praying a lot, do you pull out a dartboard in the shape of a world map? Absolutely not! There are lots of good questions to ask and things to work through as you continue to pray, become informed, and wait for God to guide you in your next steps.

You will probably find that there are some countries of the world that are not viable considerations for you for a variety of reasons. Some countries have age restrictions with either upper or lower age limits. Some restrict adoptions by single parents. There are other eligibility criteria in various countries that may restrict your ability to adopt, such as the length of your marriage, how many children you have, the gender of your children, your religion, and even your ancestry or ethnicity.

Once you have narrowed the list to the nations that you qualify to adopt from, there are other considerations regarding what those countries require. Cost may be the most crucial requirement by families seeking to adopt internationally, with the average cost of an international adoption ranging from $20,000 to more than $50,000 depending on the country. However, there are other significant requirements. For instance, many countries have a residency requirement, the time you have to be present in the country to complete the adoption. These residency requirements can range in duration from a few days to months or longer and can involve one or both parents. A full understanding of the country's *current* residency laws—not the previous experience of agencies or other adoptive families—is crucial. Though your agency may have never seen a case in which the complete residency laws were implemented, yours could be the first, and as Christians who follow the New Testament's edicts to give honor to civil authorities, you will want to be able to fully honor the laws of the country from which you plan to adopt.

This issue of honoring the laws of the country from which you intend to adopt brings me to another consideration. Although not mandatory, you may want to limit your adoption to a country that has ratified the Hague Adoption Convention. Although there is some level of debate within the transnational adoption community regarding its effectiveness, the Hague Adoption Convention is designed to protect the best interests of the child. Developed by the Hague Conference on Private International Law, the convention is a pact by nations aimed at dealing with international adoption, child trafficking, and child laundering (in which children are sold like commodities by their parents or legal caregivers). According to the text of the convention report itself, the main objectives of the convention are:

- to establish safeguards to ensure that intercountry adoptions take place in the best interests of the child and with respect for his or her fundamental rights as recognized in international law;
- to establish a system of cooperation amongst Contracting States to ensure that those safeguards are respected and thereby prevent the abduction, the sale of, or traffic in children;
- to secure the recognition in Contracting States of adoptions made in accordance with the convention.

The convention sets forth a number of principles that really clarify and standardize the adoption process within member nations. One significant bit of criticism from many in the Christian adoption movement comes regarding something within the *Subsidiarity* principle of the convention. This principle recognizes that a child should be raised by his or her birth family or extended family whenever possible. I don't think anyone would object to that provision. However, the Subsidiarity principle further states that if that type care is not possible, that other types of permanent care within the child's nation and culture are to be preferred over international adoption, but that international adoption is to be preferred over institutional care. The criticism concerns the vague nature of what the acceptable "permanent care" within a culture is. The slant of the policy seems to imply that countries should aim to prioritize preserving culture rather than to placing children in permanent loving families.

Another issue is the time that passes for many children who are held in institutional settings awaiting the potential of in-country foster-care placements that have not materialized while foreign families are prepared to receive adoption referrals. On paper, I understand the point of the Subsidiarity principle, but in practicality I feel that Hague Adoption Convention member governments should consider becoming more flexible toward placing children in loving foreign families.

Even with the questionable limitations placed by the Subsidiarity principle, the Hague Adoption Convention has the potential to solve some glaring issues by requiring:

1. adoption agencies to be accredited at the federal level;
2. an adoption services contract that spells out information about the agency's history, fees, policies, relationships, etc.;
3. a home study that meets both state and federal requirements;
4. ten hours of parent education;
5. federal approval of the adoptive parents' eligibility;
6. that the country of origin must determine that the child is adoptable within Convention consents and protections;
7. that adequate medical records be prepared and given to the prospective adoptive parents for at least two weeks review;
8. that visa applications be submitted before adoption court proceedings; and
9. that all adoption records be preserved for 75 years.

Presumably, these policies should bring about some level of safeguards in the process. Critics of the Hague Adoption Convention point out that nations must set their own compliance standards and measure their own levels of compliance. Essentially, they argue that self-policing in many nations is leading to the same levels of corruption and trafficking that existed prior to Hague. Still, I would argue that the presence of some system would be better than no system at all. You will need to inform yourself fully about the benefits and/or the risks of adopting from a Hague country versus a non-Hague country.

There are also some cultural factors that you have to consider. As I have already said, I would affirm wholeheartedly the theological notion that race and culture are of little importance to God. But they are of importance to a great many people. While I do not believe that race should be a primary consideration in an adoption, we must acknowledge that it is a consideration in the cultures both that you are bringing the child from and in the culture that you are bringing the child to join. You really need to stop and pray through the cultural and ethnic considerations of where in the world God may be leading you to go to adopt. As I said earlier, Denise and I were really open to go anywhere, and God went to great lengths to keep putting Ukraine in our path.

As I have talked with families, I have heard so many different stories of how God has led people to the nations from which they have adopted. For some it has been through a connection that has formed through years of missions trips or even through some distant connection of family heritage. Part of adopting from a culture is being ready to embrace that culture to some extent and bring it home with you. It is part of who your child is and the person she will become as she understands her story and her identity as an adolescent and adult. Make sure you can embrace that part of your child too.

Finally, you need to consider the medical conditions you are comfortable with and prepared to accept as you bring a child home. As we were traveling to adopt Erick, we saw a family who was obviously on a journey similar to ours. They were armed with medical literature and tape measures and the like. There is no way that I could know their hearts and it is not my place to judge their motivations, but I know that some of the preadoptive medical seminars that we attended in advance of our first adoption felt uncomfortably like they were slanted to help us "pick a healthy child." I am not sure that is the right perspective.

Finding your way to a child isn't like finding a car (or even choosing a puppy). You don't come up with a list of desirable options and set out to fulfill a wish list. It is important to acknowledge that these are real children with complex needs. I think you need to pray diligently on the front end and consider how willing and able you are to parent a child with physical, emotional, and social challenges, and then prepare yourself to recognize and adopt a child within those bounds. No one can know for sure what you will discover about your child during the adoption process. Getting information about physical and psychological conditions common to the region of the world you seek to adopt from will help, but you must remember this transnational adoption axiom: "In international adoption, the only thing you know for sure is that you really can't know anything for sure."

HOW TO FIND AN AGENCY

Once you have narrowed down from which country you plan to adopt, you will begin the search for an adoption agency. It's hard to overemphasize the amount of prayer and care that needs to go into this decision. The organization that will act as your agent during the adoption process is perhaps the single most significant decision you will make within the entire process and will influence so many little twists and turns along your journey. You are entering into a relationship of trust—a partnership.

Your agency will be your guide. They will be your accountability partners and your counselors. You will lean on them for advice, and you will rely on them for logistical support. They will be your eyes and ears and even your voice in a land where you likely cannot speak for yourself. They will help you to interpret a legal system that you do not know, probably will not fully understand, and may not agree with at times. They will represent you. They will be a shoulder to cry on and friends to celebrate with along the way. They will be the lap bar when the roller coaster of adoption seems too rough for you to bear. They will be there when you get home for postplacement visits. So in the in the words of Johann Wolfgang von Goethe, "Choose well. Your choice is brief, and yet endless."

The best agency will likely neither be the most economical option or the most expedient one. Frankly, this life decision is given neither to speed nor frugality. As Americans, we are conditioned to want things done quickly, efficiently, and as inexpensively as possible. Generally, what I have found in the world of transnational adoption is that when an adoption is inexpensive, many times the reason is not good for the adoptive family. I don't want this to sound overly ominous. I said that the *reason* for less expense is not good. I didn't say that it is necessarily illegal, unethical, or illegal (although it could be), but it is usually not good.

The next questions concern expediency and financial cost.

Perhaps the most significant costs in adoption are labor fees associated with the people who help in the process. These folks spend time with you learning about your family and writing reports on your behalf; coordinating your paperwork here and abroad; coordinating the logistics of the program abroad that handles the legal portion of your adoption; taking care of the logistics of your adoption trip while you are in the country, which can include everything from travel and lodging to translation and more; and following up with you once you are back home. Chances are, if you are paying an agency less, you are not receiving some of these services. It all comes down to a simple question of getting what you pay for.

To be fair, the folks who are working to facilitate adoptions deserve to be compensated fairly and justly for their work as does anyone for work accomplished. Jesus said, "And remain in the same house, eating and drinking what they provide, for the laborer deserves his wages. Do not go from house to house" (Luke 10:7). And Paul wrote, "For the Scripture says, 'You shall not muzzle an ox when it treads out the grain,' and, 'The laborer deserves his wages'" (1 Timothy 5:18). But, if you discover or suspect that the workers are being compensated exorbitantly, we all know that is not right and is a sure signal that an agency should be avoided.

Let me explain. As Denise and I adopted our three kids from Ukraine, a country in which all adoptions are independent through only one central government agency, we found that we could do more of the work ourselves and needed the services of an agency less for the second and third adoptions than for the first. I don't recommend that for most people. But I had traveled extensively in Ukraine and Eastern Europe since our first adoption, teaching as a visiting professor at Kyiv Theological Seminary and leading numerous missions teams as well as speaking to conferences for the government and for Christian organizations. I became quite comfortable being there, and we really didn't need the level of guidance that we had required in our first adoption trip. We found an agency in the US that could provide us with all of the services that our state required and could coordinate with Ukrainians who would provide the services that we needed there. For us, it was a great option, but I would gladly have done it differently if there had been a uniform set of criteria in place because Ukraine had consented to join the Hague Adoption Convention. We used the process as transparently and ethically as possible, including signing prenegotiated fee contracts with our Ukrainian adoption providers prior to beginning the adoption process, under the laws in place in Ukraine at the time.

The next questions concern expediency and financial cost. The time frame in which a transnational adoption may be completed varies dramatically from one country to the next, so we cannot properly estimate for you how long it will take. According to the documentary *Stuck*, the average cost of a transnational adoption is currently $28,000. This cost can vary by more than $10,000 depending on the country. Essentially, all agencies in a country should be working through the same legal processes. There may be some variations in the times they report, based upon areas they operate in the country and local processing times or in the sizes of their local staffs and their ability to manage a caseload, but the differences should not be that great.

Ultimately, you have to understand the countries and the legal processes in those countries and how comparable the services provided by agencies actually are. If an agency has fees that are appreciably lower than the norm but they promise comparable services, then beware. It is your responsibility to question why. If an agency promises an absurdly quick adoption timeline, they are probably involved in things at are at the least unethical if not outright illegal. If an agency is offering really economical adoption services, they are cutting corners somewhere. Those corners may be legal, but they are cutting corners nonetheless.

You must take on the task of comparing agencies and knowing whom you are deciding to work with before you start the process with them. Don't be afraid to interview them. Be prepared to ask them what they believe, what they are committed to legally and ethically, what sort of international partners they work with, and how they are accountable to those partners. You should also ask for references. Plan to interview several agencies before you make a choice. Use the Internet to gather information about agencies and ask friends and friends of friends. Compile all the data that you can. As you pray and research, the cream will rise to the surface, so to speak, and the other junk will float too. Don't become discouraged. Just skim it off and keep going. God will direct your path.

Chapter 9

What to Expect When You're Expecting on Paper: Before You Come Home

AS I HAVE SAID, THE ADOPTION PROCESS VARIES greatly from nation to nation in the transnational adoption process. While it is impossible to accurately profile all the steps in the adoption process for each individual nation, there are some commonalities to the process on the US end for many transnational adoptions. It can be helpful for us to review these to give the essence of the process.

The Hague Adoption Convention has brought some standardization to the adoption process in countries which have signed on to this international pact. This standardization gives us a bit of a framework to use as we walk through the big steps in the preadoptive process. The first step is to sign a contract with an accredited adoption agency. Agencies are accredited by the United States government to be able to provide adoptive services in Hague Adoption Convention countries. That accreditation should ensure the agency complies with a set of uniform standards that are established to promote ethical and professional conduct. If you are adopting from a non-Hague country, still ask for a contract. That contract should spell out in detail information about the agency's history, fees, policies, and relationships.

Once you have contracted with an agency, the next step is your home study.

THE HOME STUDY

I was a basket case when we were getting ready for our first home study visit. I had no idea what to expect. I have never seen our house cleaner than it was that day. We were so nervous! I don't know what I was thinking, but I guess that I expected our social worker to show up and do something that was a combination of a military white glove inspection, detective's inquisition, and essay contest. Man, was I surprised! She came over, and we really had a nice hour-and-a-half visit. We talked about ourselves, our family, our reason for adopting, and some of our expectations. She left us with a reading list and some homework, and she made appointments to visit with each of us individually for our next appointments. *Voilà!* That was it. I think we had three more visits, plus a few other things to complete such as some safety items for our house, physical exams, gathering financial records, and we were done in about 60 days. By the time we had our last home study visit for our final adoption, I don't think we even bothered to vacuum, and I am pretty sure I wore sweats. Just keeping it real!

What we found out along the way was that our social worker's job was to get to know us and to make an honest recommendation about the type of child who would best fit in our home. It was also our social worker's task to make an unbiased assessment of the fitness of our home to adapt to more children physically, psychologically, socially, and financially. While I am thankful for the other supportive roles that our social workers played for us, this is a crucial link in the chain for you as an adoptive family and for the child as a protection. When the process functions as it should, the social worker is not merely the enabler or the granter of wishes for adoptive parents, but the wise guide who will help keep you from making a mistake by taking on a child that your family is ill prepared to welcome into your family.

The requirements of an international home study can vary from country to country as well. This is where the knowledge and experience of your social worker and your agency can be invaluable. They can help you to know the exact requirements and preferred format for your country and keep you up-to-date with the changing policies and demands of your nation's process to keep you from being unduly delayed.

PARENT EDUCATION

Once your home study is under way, you can pass the time as you wait for the visits to be completed and the reports to be prepared by working on another step in the process—parent education. Ah, the parent education process. I remember it fondly. Actually, I remember some of it with the fondness of a root canal. Looking back I am really, really thankful for it, but, in the interest of full disclosure, I was an unenthusiastic participant in a great deal of it.

In 1993, when dinosaurs roamed the earth (just kidding) and the Hague Adoption Convention had yet to be ratified by the US, our social worker Barbara believed vehemently in parent education. Apparently, she believed in it much more than the Hague Adoption Convention folks because while they only mandate 10 hours of certified parent education for parents adopting from a Hague country, Barbara mandated a reading list that rivaled anything that I encountered in my PhD program

(I know I am repeating myself here, but it is still a sore subject. Bear with me. It's probably more of a cry for help!). At the end of the process, I knew more about the history and culture of Eastern Europe than the grad student who taught my freshman-level Western Civilization class, and I had become a self-proclaimed expert on bonding with a toddler. We attended more seminars on medical issues and home safety than I can count.

I guess we probably had closer to 30 to 40 hours of reading and seminars completed before we brought Erick home, and it was a great thing. We still didn't feel like we had a clue what we were doing at times, but there were fewer of those times. I know now that there were things that we did right in building bonding and attachment that we would not have known how to do without those books and seminars, and we are reaping the benefits for those things a decade later. Our parent education also taught us to seek out support and help from doctors and to use other early interventions. Those decisions paid huge dividends in language development and in other key matters.

Even if you are adopting from a non-Hague Adoption Convention country and are not required to complete preadoptive parent training, do yourself a favor and take advantage of some of the training programs that are available. I have seen a number of them that are currently available as complete online training programs with more than 20 hours of training courses. The cost of these courses may be less than one continuing education class at your local community college. That's really a bargain—and so convenient that there is really no excuse not to sign up.

Topics that you should be exposed to, either through parent education courses or through putting together your own reading and research program, include: common medical issues, attachment issues, developmental issues and schooling problems, language acquisition, cultural adjustment, problems for trauma-tized children, issues in toddler and older child adoption, effects of malnutrition, and helping your child transition and deal with grief and loss.

THE REFERRAL

However it happens from country to country, there will be a point in the process where you will get a referral and be matched to a child. If you are adopting from a Hague Adoption Convention country, sometimes the agency sends a photograph. From other countries, you may get a video. In non-Hague countries, you may not even get the referral until you are in the country meeting with a government social worker. But one way or another, you will reach this point. This is one point where Hague and non-Hague countries really differ.

It is the responsibility of the child's country to determine adoption eligibility. Each country is self-determining in how it conducts this process: how much of it is completed at the local level and how much is centralized. The process for a Hague Adoption Convention country involves identifying and determining a child's eligibility up front in the process with verifications that, at least in theory, rely more on the nation's central government than the local or regional officials. From a purely subjective view, it seems that countries which rely on more local, decentralized processes have many more problems with corruption. Local officials looking to use their offices and influence entrepreneurially can exploit transnational adoption in both subtle and explicit ways. The more explicit ways are unethical behaviors the Hague Adoption Convention attempts to address head-on: human trafficking and child laundering. The more subtle exploitation is much more common and much harder to police. It comes in the form of so-called expediency fees. These fees aren't really bribes, but they aren't really ethical either. Essentially, you aren't paying anyone to do anything that they will not normally do at some point. You are just paying them to work on a more rapid schedule. Still, these practices reek of an unseemly underbelly of questionable ethics and gray areas.

The expediency process usually goes something like this. You or your representative goes into a government office to get a document that is key to your adoption process. The document is simple and will normally take a couple of hours to produce, but you are told that the office is unusually busy at this time and they cannot accommodate your request. You will have to come back in a week and resubmit your request. After some discussion, you are told that there is another option. You can see a particular person in the office and have your case expedited for an additional fee. You see the slippery slope.

I believe that as Christ's representatives we are to avoid even the appearance of evil. We have to advocate for a system that is above reproach and refuse to engage in the slightest hint of corruption, even if we believe so passionately in the end that will come by that means. The gospel demands it!

NEXT STEPS

Once you have completed your home study and received a referral—knowing the child that you are pursuing to adopt—the focus of the journey really begins to shift. Now the paper chase really begins. At this juncture you will apply to the United States Citizenship and Immigration Service (USCIS) for approval of your eligibility to adopt. Your eligibility is based upon a review of your home study, proof of citizenship and marital status, certification that you have completed any state-mandated preadaptation requirements, and the receipt of clearance of the proper federal criminal background checks.

The process at this point is somewhat similar for both Hague and non-Hague countries. The difference is that an advance petition must be filed and approved before you can be matched with a child in a Hague country, whereas it can be accomplished after the fact when adopting from a non-Hague country. Not filing an advance petition does leave a greater potential for corruption by allowing for preselection of children outside any regulated process. By filing an advance petition, you are making a request to the US government to declare a foreign adoptee as an immediate relative. This means that upon approval, the US government agrees to the child's adoptable orphan status according to his or her home country and declares you fit to adopt the child according to the paperwork you have submitted. With this approval, you are granted permission to obtain an entry visa for the child to the US upon presenting the proper court documents and passport to give evidence of your completed adoption process in the child's home country. The form giving advance acknowledgment of the US government's approval of this petition will be made part of your adoption dossier.

THE ADOPTION DOSSIER

The adoption dossier is a set of legal documents that provides information about you to the country from which you are adopting. Essentially, it is your on-paper identity or paper trail, a detailed report with components that have been gathered throughout

They can also help you sort out which things in the medical report are reliable diagnoses and which are likely not.

the process. This required collection of documents varies from country to country, but there are some commonalities.

Assembling a dossier on your own can seem a little like a tryout for the television show *The Amazing Race*. Your agency will really earn their fee in helping you to get the format right for each and every page of this report. (And trust me; this is very, very important). Typically your dossier will need to include copies of your adoption petition, home study, birth certificates, marriage license, financial documents such as W-2s and/or tax returns, physical examination reports, copies of your USCIS petition to declare an adoptee an immediate relative, a copy of your agency's license, employment verification letters, criminal background check results, power of attorney for your agency representatives, as well as other documents the country you are adopting from might mandate. All the official forms, such as birth certificates and marriage licenses, must be certified copies. The other documents must be notarized to prove they are true and unaltered copies of the original documents and signatures.

Further, the certified copies and notarized documents must then receive an *apostille*. The apostille is an authentication performed by the secretary of state in each state to certify that the notarization is authentic. Documents have to be apostilled by the secretary of state of the state where the documents were certified or from which the notary's commission is issued. Think about it, if you and your spouse were born in different states, married in a third, and reside in a fourth, you are looking at a bit of a dizzying array of interstate document shuffling to complete the process, especially if you are under any sort of time pressure to get it all done.

Once the apostilled documents are gathered, they are usually checked for completeness by your agency. After it is determined that they are all in order, they are translated (and often the translations are certified in-country as well) and submitted by your agency to provide the basis of an adoption petition in the country from which you plan to adopt.

Although you are still a long way from finishing the process, at this point in most countries, it is time to begin to cast one eye toward the future. One way that you will want to do that is by examining your child's medical records.

MEDICAL REVIEW

The Hague Adoption Convention provides that the child's medical records must be prepared by competent authorities from his or her country and submitted to the prospective adoptive parents for at least two weeks of review before any further step in the process can be taken. This provision is designed to ensure that prospective adoptive parents are adequately informed up front about all known medical issues. It gives them the opportunity to make an informed decision about proceeding with an adoption before the process has gone too far.

Please realize that the medical records that are available on many children are not what you would expect to have in many more developed nations. The circumstances that have contributed to the adoptable status of most children have also in many cases contributed to poor or no documentation, even when they have had medical care. For a great number of children, pinpointing an exact birth date is a challenge, much less their birth weight or length. Early developmental milestones may be a mystery, and their medical records can even be filled with mystery diagnoses that will baffle trained medical professionals armed with the best journals and reference materials they can find.

An integral part of the medical review process is having the medical records examined by a competent professional. Not all physicians are equally well prepared to help. Any family medical doctor is probably well suited to complete the physicals that are necessary for your home studies and even to help you know which shots to get to prepare for your trip out of the country to get your child. But only a select few doctors in the country have the expertise to deal with the issues common to international adoptees and are familiar with the terminology used in the reports that will be coming from the various countries. These international adoption clinics can also be an integral part of your journey once you come home. We'll talk more about how to do it in the next chapter, but for now just know that establishing a relationship with one of the clinics that specialize in this is advisable at this stage in the process.

Quite a number of clinics at major hospitals and research medical centers around the United States are similar in that they are dedicated to serving the initial and continuing medical, developmental, and emotional needs of international adoptees and their families. Typically, many of the physicians and staffs from these clinics have adoption ties themselves, either as adoptive parents or as adoptees, and their passion and dedication shows. The services these clinics provide will vary some based upon personnel and expertise; but they are typically similar, offering everything from preadoption seminars; reviews of the medical reports that you receive at this part of the process; initial medical, developmental, and psychological workups when you come home; and even consultation and treatment of specific medical and behavioral challenges that may present after your child has been home with you a year or more.

There are some things that you should expect that a clinic can do for you in reviewing the medical report that you will receive as part of the adoption referral process. First, they will be able to check the report for completeness based upon what is usually expected from a particular country. If there are missing or incomplete items, they can steer you as to what to ask and how to ask it to get the rest of the information that you need to understand the child you are considering for adoption. They can also help you sort out which things in the medical report are reliable diagnoses and which are likely not.

Unfortunately, it is common to hear in transnational adoption circles that some countries have odd practices of including overdiagnoses or false diagnoses in children's medical reports. The reasons for this are unclear unless perhaps they were a way in the past of engineering a child's eligibility for adoption through special needs provisions. Whatever the reason for this practice, doctors with expertise in this area are adept at spotting the common patterns and helping you to more accurately interpret the reports and to know what to focus your attention on. They can also consult with specialists in various disciplines for more refined medical opinions, including potential treatment plans and prognoses for after you come home. Finally, they may also be able to review photos and videos for facial abnormalities and physical characteristics that may help you understand the child's developmental state and abilities.

Adopting a child with a serious, life-altering medical condition is not to be taken lightly, and it is a decision that no one can make for another. Ultimately, no one should stand in judgment of another family's decision to adopt or not to adopt based upon their ability to care for a child in light of circumstances that are learned during a medical review. The medical review process allows the family to prayerfully consider their ability to parent and provide for a child. I am not in any way suggesting that medical reviews are a way of trying to comparison shop for the ideal child or some nonsense like that. Any such notion is offensive to adoptees, adoptive parents, and even more an affront to the gospel that adoption demonstrates.

Just as learning about a child's medical or psychological difficulties during the medical review could cause a family to decide against adopting a particular child, it might solidify the family's determination to press forward with the adoption. Some of the most beautiful adoption stories I know involve children with severe physical and emotional challenges. Part of the joy and the health of those stories is that the parents knew fully of their children's needs before they adopted them, and they brought them home to both love them and give them the resources they needed to thrive.

Since the policy restricting HIV-positive adoptees from entering the US was lifted in January 2010, the number of HIV-positive children adopted into US families from abroad has risen sharply. This simple action by President Barack Obama's administration paved the way for children living with this terrible but manageable condition to be adopted and come to the US.

Part of the medical review process is not just ruling out what you *cannot* possibly do. It may also be discovering and understanding what you *can* do. No one can make the decision for you, but it is important that you get the best advice and most accurate information possible. Take the time to discover the people and resources that are available to you, and trust God to guide your decision making along the way.

> *By our third adoption trip, our luggage had shrunk considerably.*

GET READY TO GO

How you prepare yourself for your adoption travel really depends on the country from which you adopt. There is no in-country process for a few countries, and for others the process is so undefined that in-country stays of months are not out of the question. Given those extremes, I will just share a little wisdom that I have picked up after three in-country adoption journeys, each lasting between five to nine weeks in three dissimilar locations in the same country.

It is important to get everything in order as early as you can to avoid creating needless work and stress. The idea here is to make the best use of the inevitable lulls that come during the transnational adoption process. You can redeem the wait time by working ahead so that the hurried times will be less stressful. For example, make sure that your passport is up to date with a far-off expiration date.

Begin planning to receive all the immunizations required (and probably all those that are recommended) for the country where you will travel. This is especially important because several of the common travel immunizations require multiple doses for you to achieve immunity, with weeks and even months between doses. Your physician can help you with this information, or you can access it yourself through the "Traveler's Health" section of the Centers for Disease Control and Prevention (CDC) website. In some cases, you may have to provide evidence of these completed vaccinations as part of your adoption dossier or to apply for an entry visa to your child's birth country. Many of the immunizations are not routinely covered by most insurance carriers and can be quite expensive. You may be able to save a great deal of money by getting your vaccinations through your local health department instead of your primary care provider.

Also, work closely with your agency to make sure that none of your paperwork will expire while you are abroad. This would include items such as the fingerprints for the federal background checks that relate to your approval from the USCIS petition for your child's visa and other pieces of your home study and adoption dossier. These items are difficult, if not impossible, to update while you are abroad. And some related items that are part of the same process are notorious for not having the same expiration dates. Don't be afraid to verify that your agency is keeping those forms up to date by ensuring viable expiration dates as your travel date approaches. This will help you avoid a last-minute paper chase to add to your pretrip stress.

SEEK ADVICE

The wisdom and advice of those who have gone before you can be invaluable in so many ways. In the digital age, it is easier than ever to connect with people who can help you understand what your experience traveling abroad may be like. And I cannot overstate how helpful this is. I remember in 2003, when Denise and I completed our first adoption, how hard it was to get an accurate picture of what the travel conditions would be like. We trolled a couple of old LISTSERVs (electronic mailing lists) trying to pick up bits and pieces of information. Our agency gave us pamphlets and lists of what to bring that made us feel as though we were packing for a trip to the moon. I remember that Denise packed our bags—*huge* bags—weeks before the trip with everything we needed, except the few items of clothing that we were still wearing. She had neatly placed on top of each bag an itemized inventory checklist of its contents. This approach to packing turned out to be a well-planned disaster. We ended up carrying tons of things we didn't need and leaving behind a few things we wished someone had told us to bring.

How times have changed. A few weeks ago, I got an email from a complete stranger who ran across my website (rickmortononline .com) and blog. He and his family were headed to the same little obscure city where Nicholas's orphanage was, with the intention of adopting a sibling group. After reading a little of the blog, he decided to email and ask me about the town. Their adoption facilitator had never been there and had little to no knowledge of the area. We were able to trade emails and finally talk by phone. I was able to tell him a ton of things that we learned about the little town that will save them a lot of time and trouble. I gave him information about a comfortable hotel, transportation, shopping, restaurants, and so on. In some cases, it had taken us a couple of weeks to learn the things that I was able to tell him. I was so glad to be able to "pay it forward" to someone else.

By our third adoption trip, our luggage had shrunk considerably. It was amazing how we had learned to get by with a couple of pairs of dark blue jeans and an assortment of wash-and-wear accessories that could all be handwashed and air-dried easily. Take dark, wrinkle-free garments that can be layered for warmth and won't show dirt. Break in any new items before your trip, especially your shoes, and plan for comfort. Your time will be stressful enough without being uncomfortable. Don't forget to account for things like swelling of your feet on long international flights. There's nothing worse than not being able to wear your shoes at the end of a long flight! You will need all the energy and focus you have, and you will want to enjoy the experience.

Depending on where you are adopting from, you may find it more convenient and less expensive to purchase some things locally rather than to bring them, especially since airlines have increased baggage restrictions and fees. Ask about this as you interact with your agency and with folks who have adopted from the same region.

BACK UP YOUR IMPORTANT DOCUMENTS

You will want to carry backup copies for a number of important documents as you travel. For example, it may be important to have copies of the picture pages of your passports, visas (if necessary), and your dossier. My wife has a small accordion file for each of our children's adoptions that served as a document organizer for all our papers before, during, and after our journeys. While we were traveling, we kept the copies of all our documents and every receipt and piece of paperwork we received on the trip in this file.

Think about keeping electronic copies as a backup as well. A great way to do this is to take pictures of all the documents with your mobile phone camera. You will likely keep your phone with you at all times, and it can be backed up automatically to your computer and to a digital server. This provides an extra measure of security against losing track of important receipts and documents. Although copies of some documents will not suffice if the originals are lost, copies may make seeking certified replacements easier.

PLAN YOUR TRAVEL

For a while, I coordinated the enlistment office for one of the largest seminaries in the world. The task was interesting because we never really recruited anyone. We spent a lot of time sending ambassadors to open doors and praying for people and talking about our city and school, but we had two unofficial mottos. One was, "If God doesn't want you here, we don't either." (Come to think of it, that's not a bad motto for adoption.) The other was our travel motto, which also applies to adoption, "You can save the man, or you can save the money, but you can't save both."

One of the most significant out-of-pocket costs in a transnational adoption is for travel. On most adoption budgets, traveling business class internationally is out of the question. I have traveled in international business class a couple of times (because I received frequent flyer upgrades), and that will definitely help you arrive in the most rested condition, but the extra expense is really hard to justify. Rather than booking yourself the plushest seat on the plane with the best cabin service, pay more attention to the timing of your flights and your connection times. It is probably worth a little more money to get layovers that give you enough time to allow for delays (but not so much that you spend an extra half day waiting on a connecting flight). Even with all the self-booking options available via the Internet, a good travel agent can be a great (and usually free) help in sorting out these options.

Also, some airlines have special adoption fares, discounts, or rules. Travel agents who specialize in adoption, missions, and humanitarian travel can help you get the best option because all of the airlines do not treat adoptions the same. Some only offer refundable tickets at a full coach fare, while others will offer mostly refundable tickets with fairly substantial discounts off their full fares. Making sure that you are comparing tickets with similar fare rules and provisions can save you thousands of dollars. Remember that there is a built-in uncertainty about return dates for round-trip tickets because of the adoption process length in many countries.

Another good tip to save yourself a bit en route is to choose your seats well. It may seem like a small thing, but getting a seat with sufficient recline and legroom on a 12- or 14-hour flight can really be helpful. A website that has been an invaluable source of information is called Seat Guru (seatguru.com). Seat Guru has interactive seat maps for each major aircraft type worldwide with an easy-to-read, color-coded system for rating the best and worst seats on each plane. They also tell what amenities each plane has in each cabin and offer an excellent up-to-date customer review section. I highly recommend that you check this site out before you finalize your seating arrangements.

You may face the same sort of choices for in-country travel. If you are required to travel within the country once you arrive, your agency may present you with options. The "save the man or save the money" philosophy is not a bad way to think about your options here. I would pay a couple of hundred extra dollars any day to take a 1-hour flight to avoid a 14-hour train ride. Over the

Technology has changed everything.

life of the relationship with my child, that $200 seems pretty minuscule to have us better rested on the first day we spend together. Of all the purchases I may regret, that won't likely be one of them. Trust the advice of your agency, but don't be afraid to ask if there are options.

DECIDE HOW (AND HOW MUCH) TO COMMUNICATE

Chances are that you have an army of people at home who are praying for you and are anxious for updates on the progress of your adoption journey. Times have changed in the last decade. Our first adoption was at the beginning of the digital age. I remember ducking into Internet cafés to buy a few minutes to send an email home to a few folks who would send it out in a prayer chain to a group of our friends and family. We had a mobile phone that was too expensive to use except in an emergency, and we spoke to our families only sporadically. On our last adoption trip, we were traveling during Christmas and separated from our boys who stayed at home. We talked every day and even opened Christmas presents together around the Christmas tree via Skype!

Technology has changed everything, Today adoption blogs and Facebook groups have become commonplace for many families as they both chronicle their pilgrimage and stay connected to their support and prayer base at home. A couple of considerations arise as you consider how you might do this. First is the technical question: How will you gain access? As I have traveled, I am amazed about the reach of mobile technology and the Internet. From the jungles of Ecuador to the bush of Africa, mobile phones are an unremarkable part of everyday life, as is the Internet. The real issue is just figuring out how to access it affordably and securely.

Again, this is a question best posed to your agency and folks who have traveled locally, but it is something you will want to try to figure out well in advance so that you can take any adapters or equipment (including transformers and power converters) that you will need.

The second question you will need to answer is: What are you going to post, and to whom will you give access? This is a question that I would counsel you to give a lot of prayerful thought and consideration. Determine the objective for your communication. Are you communicating primarily as a journal of your experiences to chronicle your experience for yourself, your family, and possibly for others who may follow in your footsteps? A more open blog may be an option for you, although it may be to your advantage to consider a private blog that is open to only those you invite—until you have a little time to reflect and edit the post for more public consumption. Is your journal more of a prayer journal to update a close circle of family and friends? Consider an invitation-only Facebook group that will allow posting of comments, photos, videos, and so on.

The downside of using social media sites like Facebook is their propensity to change privacy policies that can impact who could have access to your information. A social media account like Facebook is a great option because it is easy to set up and easy to update, but you must not ignore the terms and conditions that these accounts are set up under and how those stipulations change over time as you leave an account active with them. Your story and your child's story is too precious to put at risk by sloppy blogging or bad Internet practice. I can't tell you the number of times I have cringed over the years reading an adoption blog where a very well-meaning adopting/adoptive parent has poured his or her guts out on an open blog about something that should probably have best been left for the privacy of a trusted group of prayerful friends and family or a support group at church. Yet, there the story stands indelibly etched in cyberspace, unable to be retracted. There is a balance that we have to find between being authentic and seeking help and not creating a legacy of greater damage for our children.

You also have to be careful about how and when it is appropriate to share the name(s) and pictures of your child(ren). Your agency can advise you, but to do this too soon can actually violate the law in many countries and complicate your adoption process. Also, please be careful in sharing information about other children that you may meet as you may be unwittingly violating privacy laws and exposing children to harm from traffickers and others with insidious agendas.

AS YOU GO

When it comes to the actual trip to go and get your child, I think I can sum up many of the conversations that I have had with other transnational adoptive parents with Charles Dickens's opening line from *A Tale of Two Cities,* "It was the best of times, it was the worst of times." The trip to bring home a child is a monumental but difficult step in your journey. Knowing and being prepared is half the battle with the rest being spiritually prepared.

I don't mean to cast a long, dark shadow over what really can be a joyful experience, but I must be transparent in telling you that lots of families will testify that their trips were anything but joyous in the moment. Travel stresses, jet lag, cultural adjustments, traveler's stomach, and so much more, can conspire to complicate the process. With all that is going on around you and in you, it is perfectly natural that your emotions may be on edge and you may be feeling more stress than normal. To compound things, you are totally out of your element. The phone calls you could make at home to take care of problems don't help: You have no legal standing in the country from which you are adopting. You are a guest at the invitation of the government, and you are at its mercy. Likely, you don't even speak the language, so you can't advocate for your waiting child or yourself and that, in and of itself, is stressful. On top of it all, you probably can't stroll down to the corner market to get your favorite comfort food. It can all be a little disconcerting, especially when things don't go as expected and, believe me, they probably won't always go as expected.

This is one of the reasons why choosing an agency you trust is so important. At times when you are tired, stressed, and disconcerted, they will help you and protect you in ways that you may not even fully understand in the moment. They are familiar with the local laws and customs. They can help you to know when to act and when to sit tight.

The trip home can be tough too. You might think that this would be an easy trip, especially if your child is coming out of a difficult institutional environment. Instead, try to see the trip from the child's perspective. The child is being whisked away from the safety and security of what is known (even if the known is bad) to the unknown. If the child is coming from an institution, his or her days are built on routine and predictability. Not only are you shattering that predictability, but you are doing it predicated on very little relationship and with language barriers. The child is likely going to have periods of sensory overload. The onslaught of new sights, sounds, and smells will be overwhelming.

As parents are rounding the corner toward home, they see home as the prize. It's the light at the end of the tunnel. What for you represents the end of the journey in comfort, familiarity, family, friends, your bed, etc., represents a whole new world to your child. In so many ways, that is a great thing, but it can also be a difficult and intimidating thing. The sprint to get home is not the end of the journey of your adoption. It is the end of the introduction. You are now really beginning the first chapter of your story.

Take some simple advice from someone who has been there three times. Slow down and keep your trip simple. I would even be careful about things like the airport at home. A lot depends on your child, his or her age, development, background, and so on, but simple is better. Likely, there will be a lot of people who will have been invested in praying for you and following your journey, and they will want to welcome you home. Don't feel undue pressure to put your child (or yourself) in a stressful circumstance of meeting everyone at the same time, especially at the airport.

We gave in a little bit with Nicholas and had a pretty big group of folks meet us at the airport. As soon as we entered the terminal, I knew it was a mistake. After 24 straight hours of travel, he totally shut down. He was in complete sensory overload. All around him there were "Welcome Home" signs and gifts and toys and hugs. Folks were really thoughtful and amazing, but it was just too much for him. He was the kid that was roaring with laughter at the ice dispenser in a fast-food restaurant just a couple of hours earlier during our first layover in the US. Everything was new to him, and he was the life of the party. When we got home, he hit the wall. We were reminded a little that day to keep it simple and close to home and give our new family a little time to adjust and bond.

Nevertheless, it was good to be home and to begin writing the first chapter of his story in our family. When everyone was gone and we closed the door behind us, reality began to set in once again.

We were home. Real life was just beginning.

Chapter 10

Once You Come Home

WITH NEWBORNS, WE ALL UNDERSTAND THE importance of bonding and attachment. In adoption, it is important that your family take the time to bond even if your kids are older. Granted, that bonding may look and feel very different, but it is no less important.

With our first adoption, we had read enough books on attachment and toddler adoption that we became extremely conscious of bonding. After we came home, we spent about six weeks hiding out as a family. When our little Erick got fed, changed, comforted, put to sleep, bathed, or pretty much anything else, Momma or Daddy did it. Other than some trips out to the pediatrician and visits by some early intervention therapists, we focused on getting off to a good start with each other, punctuated with a few weekend visits by the grandparents. Even then, we made sure that the grands knew that it was important for us to take a primary role in Erick's care and security.

In those early days, he really didn't have a lot of stranger anxiety, and we knew that was a product of the environment he had been living in for a while. It was important for him to have consistent care from the same folks to learn that he could trust us and feel safe. Before long, he did. I'll never forget seeing it for the first time. In the beginning, he was always a little *stiff* when you held him. He always held his head up and kept his distance. I remember one afternoon seeing Denise pick him up and watching as he put his head on her shoulder and his little body just relaxed and formed to hers. It was as if when she picked him up, he exhaled with his whole body and said, "I trust you, Momma!" It was powerful.

With older kids, you will earn their trust differently. It takes more time, so you need some time to focus on getting to know them to be able to get off to a good start. With both of our older kids, we kept them home several weeks before starting them in school. The time at home was good for bonding and good to give them one-on-one time with their mom while the rest of the family was at school and work. Trust building takes a lot longer with most older kids, particularly if they are coming from hard places. We just have to be there and be consistent.

Churches can help during these early days of bonding in some practical ways. We are quick to take meals to families with newborns as they are adjusting to a new addition. Why not do the same for an adoptive family? Be sure to respect the family's need for privacy and routine, but a couple of weeks of provided meals can be a lifesaver as a family is adjusting to its new addition from abroad.

COMMON ISSUES AND EXPECTATIONS

Medical Issues

The conditions that many orphans live in make them susceptible to a wide variety of health concerns, and some are institutionalized as a direct result of their health issues. These health issues can range all the way from minor things like lice, scabies, and parasites to major medical or psychological concerns. The five most common major health issues related to transnational adoptions are hepati-

> *Reactive attachment disorder (RAD) means that the child has great difficulty forming loving relationships that endure.*

tis B, HIV, fetal alcohol spectrum disorder (FASD), reactive attachment disorder (RAD), and sensory integration dysfunction (SID).

Hepatitis B infections are common in Asia, South America, Eastern Europe, and some parts of Africa. Many orphans from these regions have been infected with hepatitis B from birth and struggle to be adopted because of their health status. Most of these children will live a long and healthy life, and a hepatitis B diagnosis need not cause undue alarm or halt an adoption process. The Hepatitis B Foundation (hepb.org) is an excellent resource for prospective adoptive families to help them understand this disease and what it would mean to bring home a child with it.

The HIV/AIDS pandemic has ravaged children in Africa, especially in the sub-Saharan portion of the continent. Traditionally, extended families have cared for orphans in this region of the world, but the sheer mass of the crisis has overwhelmed many, and the death of a grandparent can quickly result in a circumstance where there is no one to care for a child. To make matters worse, the prejudice and social isolation of an orphan who has lost a parent to AIDS can be horrible. The indigence and separation that results can leave them vulnerable to contracting HIV themselves. In actuality between 20 to 40 percent of the children born to mothers with AIDS actually acquire the virus, although a child can test positive for 12 to 15 months after birth without actually being positive. Whether they contract HIV from their parent or as a result of lifestyle, an orphan with HIV is certainly one of the very "least of these." As HIV therapies continue to be refined, many families are adopting children with HIV and bringing them home to lead healthy, happy lives.

Fetal alcohol spectrum disorder (FASD) is a cluster or pattern of related health issues that are associated with binge drinking by a birth mother or with constant low-level alcohol exposure by the developing child throughout the prenatal period. FASD is more common in Eastern Europe and less common in Asia. There are certain physical features common to children suffering with FASD, including thin upper lip and small eyelid openings, a sunken nasal bridge with a small upturned nose, smooth skin between the nose and upper lip, small teeth, and a small head circumference with a smaller than average brain size. There may also be other physical deformities to the joints, limbs, or fingers; heart defects; and slow growth either prenatally or after birth. Additionally, common behaviors include severe intellectual impairment and delayed development, short attention span, hyperactivity, poor impulse control, extreme nervousness, and anxiety. Doctors specializing in international adoption medicine can often diagnose the signs of FASD from photos and videos along with medical and developmental records. This information can be invaluable in helping you to plan as you consider adopting a child who may have very special needs as a result of FASD.

Reactive attachment disorder (RAD) means that the child has great difficulty forming loving relationships that endure because the child has never formed a bond of trust with a parent or primary caregiver. Often RAD is exacerbated by underlying abuse and neglect. Typically, these traumatic experiences can be traced back to the early, formative years of a child's life. This is the bad news. The good news is that ample evidence exists that God has wired us as resilient creatures capable of enduring much hurt and experiencing much healing. Consistency and loving care can break through all that hurt. Techniques and therapies exist to build trust, reduce anxiety, and promote attachment. Ultimately, our goal is simple. We want these kids to learn to trust us as loving and consistent parents, so that one day they will find it credible that a loving heavenly Father sent His Son as a way for them to be reconciled to Him.

Part of the normal task of infancy is that children explore their world in safety and security. As they discover the world through their senses, infants and toddlers are constantly in the process of integrating what they discover into their developing thinking. When a child's development is hindered by poverty, disease, neglect, or institutionalization, it can be difficult for them to integrate what they sense into how they think. As a result, the body may overreact or underreact to stimuli such as sound or temperature, or the child may substitute a violent act, such as headbanging, for the need to be rocked to sleep by a loving caregiver. This is a sensory integration dysfunction (SID). Therapy strategies can help to *rewire* the brain and help to account for learning differences.

Educational and Language Development Issues

Language development and education can be significant issues for transnational adoptive families as well. Commonly, children coming from underdeveloped countries and from institutional environments will be behind educationally and developmentally. For instance, as a general rule, you can assume for every three months that a child is institutionalized, that child will experience one month of delayed growth physically, socially, emotionally, and/or intellectually. To compound matters, most of the children adopted transnationally will not initially speak the language of their new country. So, language acquisition and development can complicate early assessment, and intervention will be needed to help a newly adopted child to acquire a new language well and to maximize his or her potential to learn. While most school systems provide English as a second language (ESL) programs and other interventions to help children with developmental delays, they are most often not equipped to deal with the complexities of a child with both challenges, particularly in discriminating which of the child's conditions are related to language acquisition and which are not. So it is important to seek a full developmental assessment from a qualified professional through an international adoption clinic accustomed to working with children who have been adopted transnationally. This will ensure that you are positioning your child to receive all of the services he or she needs as quickly as possible. State and federal law provide for a great deal of this help through federally mandated early intervention and special education programs. Also, some therapy and intervention services may be covered by private health insurance. Do your homework to know the laws of your state and the provisions of your health insurance. You will be your child's best advocate in receiving the services he or she is entitled to receive.

Language development is a complex process. For very young children, it is pretty straightforward, although you may note a *mute* period where they stop babbling and listen a lot. Babbling is a language-specific stage children use to practice the sounds that are necessary to speak the language we hear around us. Usually the young child will just start talking. Sign language may be helpful in the interim, but don't worry, the words will come. For older children who are not yet writing, their language acquisition will be an almost complete swap. They, too, will have a mute period followed by an explosion of words coming seemingly dozens at a time. As quickly as they are acquiring the new language, they will lose the old one. For older children who have learned to write in their native language, as long as they continue to practice, they will not lose it. However, learning a new language is more difficult for them. Experts say that it takes seven to ten years for an adolescent or adult to reach fluency in a new language.

Psychological Issues

The psychological issues familiar to transnational adoptees are most often a result of trauma, abuse, neglect, or stress from changes in circumstances and environment. The issues most often mentioned by parents and adoption advocates are developmental delays, stress disorders (including post-traumatic stress disorder, or PTSD), sleep problems, and anxiety. The developmental delays, sleep problems, and anxiety are generally symptoms of other medical or psychological problems, including the aforementioned stress disorders. Getting to the root of these issues can involve multiple underlying medical and psychological issues contributing to those that are coming to the surface. If you are the parent of a child who is grappling with psychological issues that are manifesting themselves, and you are struggling through understanding and addressing them, you have to remember what brought your child to this place. The child didn't ask to be where she is, and her responses are the result of some really tough experiences. Also, she didn't get here overnight, and healing probably won't come quickly.

Stress disorders come in varying degrees. PTSD is the recognized disorder in this spectrum because of its identification with traumatized military combat veterans from conflicts such as the Vietnam War. PTSD and traumatic stress are not the same thing. PTSD is a very specific disorder that impedes a person's functioning over time through flashbacks, recurring and intrusive recollections of the traumatic event, difficulty concentrating, a magnified startle response, and dramatic avoidance behaviors.

Most abused and neglected orphans, though they may be suffering greatly, are not suffering from PTSD. The traumatic stress that plagues them is hurtful and runs deep. It may come out in unexpected ways. Often stress from underlying past trauma can come out as immature behaviors, periods of sadness and crying, poor concentration, fears of personal harm, aggressive behaviors, withdrawal/social isolation, attention-seeking behavior, anxiety, and irrational fears. Under stress, behaviors that were outgrown come back (bedwetting, fear of the dark, speech difficulties, clinging and whining, and separation anxiety). Recognizing the signs of traumatic stress and seeking out a mental health professional familiar with traumatic stress and the treatment of children is crucial.

IT TAKES A VILLAGE . . . AND A CHURCH

Extended family, church, school, and others, such as doctors and counselors, can all play a vital supporting role with a family and paint a beautiful picture of the body of Christ as they work together. In particular, the church can really help families by seeking out these resources, identifying them, and making them available to families. This could be a great ongoing project for a team of people within the orphan ministry of your church.

There are also ways for resource professionals in your community to help adoptive families. The TCU Institute for Child

Development offers advanced training for doctors, counselors, social workers, and teachers in the Trust Related Behavioral Interventions (TRBI)

> *Let the families take the lead.*

model, and there are scholarships available to help some of these professionals get training to be able to help adoptive families.

Additionally, international adoption clinics can provide testing and developmental assessments to help guide the treatment and intervention plans of local doctors, therapists, and teachers who may not be used to seeing the complex issues common to children adopted transnationally. Over the years, adoption clinics have been formed at most of the major children's hospitals in the United States. Having had experience with a couple of these clinics, I would recommend taking your child for at least a full initial workup that you can give to your local doctors, teachers, and therapists to provide them greater insight into preparing a plan to help your child adjust and develop well.

Churches also need to think through how to help and support adoptive families once they are home. If we know that responding to James 1:27 in larger and larger numbers will mean that more families will adopt, then we must help as a community. We can't simply call families to act and then stand aside as institutions. The implications are significant. Churches have to change. Churches have to anticipate adapting preschool, children's, and student programming to children with language deficits, sensory issues, and developmental delays. This may mean placing children in developmentally appropriate settings for discipleship; giving them more individualized attention; and adapting curriculum, games, or social events for cultural, developmental, or language differences. One way that our current church has helped is through a bimonthly program called Recess, a respite program that targets families with children with special needs. Children are invited to the church for a fun night of games, movies, food, Bible stories, crafts, and so on. Each child has a buddy that gives him or her undivided attention for the evening, and all of the activities are adaptable according to the child's needs. Siblings are welcome too, so Mom and Dad get a night off to relax or have a date night. Several of our adoptive families have found this program to be a great encouragement.

Churches also have to create support communities where parents can share struggles and victories in a safe place, learn from each other, and find community with people with whom they share a great deal. In addition to pointing people to good resources and help, we need to create safe places for adoptive families to unburden themselves. As I have said, adoption can be hard at times, and sometimes, you are not OK. I think some of our theological rhetoric gets in the way of admitting that. Yes, adoption is a picture of the gospel, but we are not God. He is a perfect parent, and we are not. Dealing with our own brokenness and our children's in this process can be downright nasty at times, but we are not hopeless and we are not alone. God is with us, and so should the church be.

We need to create structures in the church that help adoptive families feel the love of God through being loved and supported by us. We meet each week with such a group in our church. The group started off formally; we began by watching a video series to help us improve connecting with our kids who have come from hard places. We continued because we built community. It is safe. We help each other. We cry together. We say things to each other that we would never say in front of other people because we know we will not be judged. We ask silly questions because we know the others in this group will not think they are silly. We go to each other's birthday parties because we don't have to explain the awkwardness of extended families that may include a birth mother or others not in the adoptive family. It just works and, if your church has families who are fostering and adopting, I would encourage you to start a support community. The group does not have to be anything too formal or structured. Let the families take the lead. They will shape it into something that will be great. Only insist that it is open, that it cares for people, and that it honors the gospel, and you cannot go wrong.

In every adoption the formation of *home* is the goal, but home is something that has to be built. As with anything worthwhile, building a home with a transnationally adopted child will take time and effort, and it may not look like the fairy tale that many might imagine before adopting, but it is worth it. If you choose adoption, I pray that God will bless you and give you a great story of your transformation and your child's for His glory.

Where Do We Go from Here?

AS YOU HAVE SEEN, THE RUMBLINGS OF A GLOBAL movement are reverberating all around us. God is moving in His church on behalf of the fatherless in a special way. The past half decade in particular has been amazing, as we have watched God pour out His Spirit all over the world, catalyzing a response by the local and global church. So the natural question becomes, not coincidentally, the title of this conclusion: Where do we go from here? There are a few things that each of us must do:

Continue to humble yourself and pray. God is the author and the source of this movement. Ultimately, it is for His glory and His namesake even as it is for the good of orphans all over the globe. We can never forget that. No matter how good we think we have become at understanding the crisis or how adept we have become at addressing it, we cannot forget that we are not the source of the orphans' ultimate help. We are wholly dependent on God, and we must call out continually for His help. Take time to pray strategically for nations. Set aside unhurried and unhindered time to dwell in prayer for orphans.

Keep learning. It seems that the more time I spend in a place in the world, the less I know about it. The deeper I come to know a place and a people not my own, the more I tend to appreciate the depth and complexity of their lives and culture. As we seek to come alongside the nations of the world and help them solve their orphan issues, we have to continue to learn from them and with them.

Don't grow weary in well doing. At times the work is hard and the things we see are downright horrific, but it is good to persevere. The gospel demands that we endure so that the work of re-creation and reconciliation we accomplish points people toward ultimate restoration in the Savior. We know the end of the story. The King returns and establishes His kingdom, and we have an inheritance with Him. It's guaranteed! Some days the work only has joy because we have assurance of the final outcome, and it has fulfillment because we have an inheritance that can't be nullified.

Support national movements and national leaders, respecting what God has given them in gifts, talents, abilities, and potential, and trusting them to emerge as the servant leaders that God has ordained them to be.

I look forward in another half decade to looking back on what God has done!

COMMANDED TO CARE
Other resources by this author on the topic of orphan care

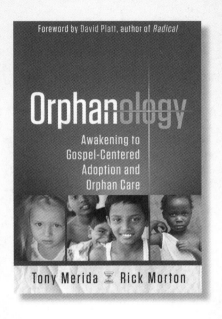

Orphanology
Awakening to Gospel-Centered Adoption and Orphan Care

TONY MERIDA AND RICK MORTON

ISBN 13: 978-1-59669-302-9 • ISBN 10: 1-59669-302-9 • N114137 • $14.99

Visit NewHopeDigital.com for additional resources surrounding this topic such as:

- A Digital Bible Study to Accompany the Book
- 9 Ideas for Small-Group Ministry to Widows and Orphans
- Digital Art Forums
- 5 Questions to Ask Before Adopting
- Video Interviews with the Author

Available in bookstores everywhere. For information about these books or our authors, visit NewHopeDigital.com. Experience sample chapters, podcasts, author interviews, and more! Download the New Hope app for your iPad, iPhone, or Android!

WorldCrafts℠ develops sustainable, fair-trade businesses among impoverished people around the world. Each WorldCrafts product represents lives changed by the opportunity to earn an income with dignity and to hear the offer of everlasting life.

Visit WorldCrafts.org to learn more about WorldCrafts artisans, hosting WorldCrafts parties and to shop!

WORLDCRAFTS℠
Committed. Holistic. Fair Trade.
WorldCrafts.org 1-800-968-7301